Seeking Wholeness

Insights into the Mystery of Experience

Roland Evans

SunShine Press Publications

SunShine Press Publications, Inc.
P. O. Box 333
Hygiene, CO 80533
Web: www.sunshinepress.com
Email: sunshinepress@sunshinepress.com

Artwork, "Days of Creation" by Jessica
Cover design by Laura Woods

Publisher's Cataloging-in-Publication Data
(Provided by Quality Books, Inc.)

Evans, Roland.
    Seeking wholeness : insights into the mystery of experience
    / Roland Evans. – 1st ed.
    p. cm.
    Includes bibliographical references and index.
    LCCN: 2001086070
    ISBN: 1888604182

    1. Transpersonal pyschology.   I. Title.

BF204.7.E93 2001   150.19'8
                                QBI00-1094

Printed in the United States
5 4 3 2 1
Printed on recycled acid-free papers using soy ink

Dedication

To Orianne, Emanuel and Marisha,
and to the memory of Winifred Rushforth, OBE, MB, ChB,
(1885-1983), pioneer of the Spirit.

The way to God is not like the ways in this world,
which you can tread with your feet.
The way to God can be traversed by human beings
only when their whole body, their whole self,
has been awakened and is alive and understands
how God's power is.
—Bapak Muhammad Subuh Sumohadiwidjojo

Acknowledgements

Without the patience and love of my wife, Orianne, this book would never have happened.

Thank you to: Jerry Ruhl for your constant support and good advice, Halim Berrier for essential testing, Allan Combs for warm encouragement, Diana Martin for editing and suggestions.

Thanks to all my clients who have patiently educated me in the ways of therapy.

Thanks to the students of Naropa University who have kept me interested in what I teach.

Three wayang spirits, moving in a powerful dance of life, loaned me the energy to complete what I only half understand.

A final appreciation to T. S. Eliot who, in his Four Quartets, has eloquently voiced what I struggle to express.

Confidentiality Statement

Many clients have kindly given permission for details of their therapy to be used in my writing. To protect confidentiality all names have been changed. Also, I have blended information from a number of different people and sources so that any particular individual is difficult to recognize. If one of the dreams or stories is yours, please forgive me for any unintended offense.

Contents

Foreword

What a wonderful gift Roland Evans has offered us. In this book he casts his net wide and pulls in many stars. He dares to ask the "big questions" of life, concerns that we ponder at 3 A.M., in times of turbulent transition or quiet repose, questions like: What kind of life is worth living? Why am I suffering, and what should I do? How do I know what is the right decision?

In *Seeking Wholeness*, Roland gives us a guide for living. He challenges us to see in fresh ways. We might call it process psychology, a set of tools for approaching experience as a moving, ever-changing flow, a movie rather than a series of still photos. This way of understanding life as a flowing, interconnected system is part of a new paradigm that has emerged in many different disciplines—physics, biology, ecology, economics, philosophy, even organizational management.

Seeking Wholeness is one of the first books to apply these new ideas to psychology in a comprehensive manner. Family systems therapy has, since its inception, been informed by such thinking, but this book applies a systems perspective in new and exciting ways to explore intrapsychic phenomena and the transpersonal realm. As such, it is essential reading for therapists, counselors and healers of all varieties.

While Roland's work is brimming with ideas, it also remains open to mystery, wonder, and awe. At its core *Seeking Wholeness* is guided by and infused with an intense spirituality. This is psychology that fully embraces the depth of psyche and does not artificially cordon itself off from cosmological concerns. By showing us practical strategies for bringing the sacred into daily life, it provides rich food for the heart and the soul. You don't need to be in the helping professions to understand and benefit from this book—anyone interested in cultivating inner growth and integrity will benefit from the stories and exercises contained within.

I first met Roland in Boulder, Colorado, a decade ago, and I was intrigued by the originality of his mind but even more impressed by his essential aliveness. I believe that he is a masterful therapist in large part because he embodies what Carl Rogers called *congruence*, the capacity to be fully oneself. You too will get a taste of that in the beauty and inspiration of stories from the author's surprising and unconventional life.

This is a book to be savored, lived with, and returned to again and again to help deepen the experience of your own life journey. Enjoy.

—Jerry M. Ruhl, Ph.D., Licensed Psychologist and co-author of *Contentment* with Robert Johnson

Preface

Except for the point, the still point,
There would be no dance, and there is only the dance.
I can only say, there we have been: but I cannot say where.
And I cannot say, how long, for that is to place it in time.
—T. S. Eliot (from *Burnt Norton*)

Each of us must find out who we are and where we are going. You could say this has been the underlying theme of my life. It seems to have started with my early attempts to understand a bewildering home life. Although not particularly traumatic, my family experience was odd; it certainly did not fit the normal social molds.

My parents were separated, so as a young child living in Wales I spent most of the time with my mother and five siblings in cramped public housing. We were poor, though not deprived. My mother worked, but also stole chickens and vegetables from farms and gardens around the district—including those belonging to my wealthy grandparents. To put it simply, she was headstrong and difficult.

Weekends and holidays we children would go to Ffrwdgrech, my grandparent's country estate. There we slept in the 'night nursery' near the nanny, played hide and seek throughout the 35 rooms of the mansion, and could walk all day and still be on the family land. My grandparents were restrained and somewhat Victorian in their manner, quietly disapproving of our childish exuberance. My unassuming father came whenever he could get away from his work on a distant farm.

The transition from chaos to ordered calm, from poverty to faded luxury, from tight 'council house' to endless spaciousness was strange, yet taken for granted. It left a question mark around who I was supposed to be.

This question extended into the rest of my life. We children went to a convent school run by Irish nuns in a small Welsh town where Catholics were very much the separate minority. Within that school, we were the only children who were nominally protestant—my grandparents being upper-class Anglicans. So although I learned my catechism and went to mass on Holy Days, I was the one left sitting while my friends went up to the altar rail for communion.

I was never sure whether I was Irish and Catholic because I was born in Ireland, or Welsh and protestant because my father's family came from Wales. This was very important for my early sense of identity—to be able to say who I was and where I came from. Wherever I found myself I was not sure I belonged; I was always on the fringe, somewhat of an outsider.[1]

The urgent dilemma of, "Who am I? What am I supposed to be?" intensified in late adolescence. On the small rugged Irish farm where I lived and worked, yearning for something more profound, I would look out across the westerly waters of Bantry Bay. The sunsets were rich and extravagant—wild banners of changing color and light framing rocky headlands and bleak islets. I wanted desperately to hold that beauty, to hear what it was trying to tell me. Something vibrated deep inside me, gouging out space for experience. It is hard to imagine anything more grand, more expansive, yet more transient. Then the sunset was gone and soft dusk would fall.

I began to sense the inner mystery of being human that cannot be expressed. Trapped on the outside of life, I could feel a reality just beyond my grasp, hidden behind an obscuring veil. I wanted to know and experience the mystery, to capture whatever hides behind our five senses. But I couldn't get in deep enough.

Later, I thought studying psychology at Edinburgh University might offer some insight, but was quickly disillusioned. Academic psychology's dogmatism was oppressive, determined to dismantle the human being into pieces—bits of cognition and affect, personality traits, stimulus and response. None of that came close to capturing the texture of my experience. Consciousness, spirituality, creativity, communion—all the things important to me were ignored or relegated to a back ward of crazy and irrelevant ideas.

I remember my excitement at accidentally discovering *systems thinking*. Here at last was an antidote to reductionism. Writers such as Arthur Koestler and Gregory Bateson, with their emphasis on relationship and wholeness, gave me hope that there might be a different way of understanding my own experience.[2] But they also seemed too constricted by the rules of scientific logic and rationality to contain the whole of what is humanly possible.

Training as a psychologist, I became resigned to the fact that there was no adequate model of human experience. The theories behind therapy made little sense. They seemed to emanate from a parallel universe, totally different from the one I live in. Certainly I could never get my clients to fit the diagnostic boxes; each person seemed too unique and complex.

It took me a long time to remember something fundamental: I had come to psychology through spirituality, not through rational decision. At eighteen I joined Subud, an international spiritual organization.[3] Its spiritual exercise, the latihan, has been the mainstay of my life and a reliable source of guidance ever since. Inner promptings and synchronistic events steered me toward psychotherapy. I knew it was 'right' for me.

Yet when working with my clients, I excluded this whole transpersonal dimension of knowing.[4] I believed that, while helping others, I should keep my most central understandings and experiences hidden.

Like most psychologists I was taught not to contaminate psychotherapy practice with my private concerns. This 'rule' is put in place to protect clients from proselytizing or from self-indulgent therapists who use others to satisfy their own needs. It is important, but often gets interpreted narrowly, that the only correct way to help others is to keep at a distance and use simplistic models of human beings.

For years I kept the two ways of knowing—rationality and mystery—tidily separated. Yet this was not true for the people coming to consult me. They were encouraged to express and experience all aspects of their being and my task was to help them. Eventually I was forced to recognize my double standard: how could I exhort my clients toward wholeness if I remained split in myself.

I see now that every person walks into my office "trailing clouds of glory", as Wordsworth says so beautifully. Welcome or not, spiritual experiences and metaphysical questions are constantly present. We are all human and so we are looking for answers that create inner meaning and completeness. The transcendent cannot be wrenched away from the personal. Psychology and spirituality are different vistas, complementary perspectives on the same path. We need the insights of both to understand our humanness as best we can.

In my work, I sense that what makes us human can never be fully captured. We swim through our lives as in a depthless ocean. Only a part which is self-aware rises above the surface. The great bulk of our being is submerged—working hard to keep us afloat and in motion. All is fluid and ever-changing and we are flowing and changing with it.

It is the flowing nature of our experience that I address here. I seek to reconcile the mysterious with the obvious, to connect the multitude of threads of our humanity. These words join your experience with mine. As with all relationship, there is something trying to happen beneath and beyond the known. Perhaps you can extract what you need out of these pages and weave your own tapestry of meaning. Perhaps you will begin to see the obvious in a slightly different light. And perhaps some story will evoke a way of knowing that goes beyond words, that is vital and alive. This is my hope.

When you live in the Irish countryside, there are those days when the mist and drizzle sets in. The landscape softens and all is drenched. This is a "fine soft day" for the farmer. The shape of the world is shrouded; everything seems closer, all sense of distance erased. Sometimes the light changes and colors fluoresce. No green is as vivid as an Irish green; no yellow vibrates so intensely. On such days life slows. Only essentials are attempted as the damp penetrates everything. It is time to huddle around the turf fire with a cup of tea. It is time to engage in a conversation that seeks to penetrate the enigma of our human experience.

Introduction

For in fact what is man in nature?
A Nothing in comparison with the Infinite, an All in comparison with the Nothing, a mean between nothing and everything.
—Blaise Pascal

To be human is difficult. We are not unified beings, not yet whole. Stretched between the finite and the infinite, human beings are complex creatures of many dimensions, filled with paradox and an inclination for self-deception. We often fall short of our highest hopes and aspirations, forget ourselves in the rush to accomplish everyday tasks. Yet even when captured by the urgent demands of the material world, we still hunger to find meaning for our life experience. Parts of our being seem narrow and inflexible, yet other parts are glorious, limitless.

How are we to live fully—become what we aspire to? Is it possible? Some few humans show us what can be attained. Mahatma Gandhi, a great soul, tells us, "I have not the shadow of a doubt that any man or woman can achieve what I have, if he or she would make the same effort and cultivate the same hope and faith."[1]

This is a powerful challenge. We may discount Gandhi's words by assuming that he, unlike you and I, was born exceptional. That is not so. He was, in fact, somewhat limited: "There was nothing unusual about the boy Mohandas Karamchand Gandhi, except perhaps that he was very, very shy. He had no unusual talents, and went through school as a somewhat less than average student."[2] As a young lawyer he made a fool of himself with his inability to speak up in court. Yet this tiny and timid young man became one of mankind's great spiritual and political leaders.

Gandhi provides a model for our aspirations—to reach beyond limitations toward wholeness. Occasionally, in our ordinary lives, we sense that there is more than we can see or touch, that we are part of some greater pattern.[3] We feel it in nature, in the abundance of living organisms that share our planet. We see it in the exquisite beauty of galaxies and stars expanding across the universe. As we recognize our particular corner of this greater pattern, a portion of the extraordinary orderliness of the universe, we know we are involved in a mysterious, unfolding evolution.

We have our part to play in that evolution. As human beings we can choose to embrace or neglect our own growth. Difficulties and deprivations create stuck patterns in our being, constriction in what we allow ourselves to experience. Without noticing, we become trapped in a backwater of our personality, unable to grow into new and unfolding forms. Yet one different experience can unexpectedly set us free.

In my twenties, a friend made a passing comment, "You know, you take yourself too seriously." His words resonated through my being, jostling my view of myself. Abruptly, I realized I was growing old before my time, ensnared by some warped idea of maturity. His casual comment helped shift the rigidity that was slowly squeezing joy out of my life.

Can you recognize the patterns that keep you entangled? Do you know yourself well enough to find the shape and meaning of your whole being? These are essential questions that are impossible to answer without assistance. When we stop and get quiet inside we find the help we need—a flowing vibration of inner vitality. This is the *Life Force* that imbues all existence with life and movement.

It is hardest to experience this vibration when we are busy and tense, or if our mind is too active. Because we get so involved in the outer aspects of our lives, we seldom notice what we are missing, or see the restrictions we imposed on ourselves. Looking for excitement, for an adrenaline high, for the satisfaction of power and control, we become engrossed with the shadow of experience, not its substance. We sense something is missing, but we are not sure where to look. What we have mislaid is an essential connection with ourselves and our experience.

All life seeks connection—the more connectivity the more alive and complete. The movement toward connection and wholeness is universal. Carl Rogers, the founding father of counseling, calls this, "the actualizing and formative tendency." It generates an inner urgency toward self-awareness and growth.[4] We can rely on this flowing principal to support our journey through life. As Sam Keen eloquently tells us in his *Hymns to an Unknown God*, "We are in transit toward an unknown destiny."[5]

From this perspective we begin to ask different questions about our experience. Instead of, "Why am I discontented and unhappy?" we ask, "How am I stuck; what parts of my being are disconnected; how can I become more whole; am I fulfilling the purpose of my life?"

These questions require we search within, not outside of ourselves for the answers. As we delve deeper, a different way of understanding arises. Unhappiness is the end result of many pathways. Childhood losses and betrayals, disappointments, life crises, and physical illness—all these can be hindrances to our well being. But these personal difficulties do not explain our deepest dissatisfaction.

If we neglect to become the most that we can, ignore the voice within that keeps asking, "Is this all there is to life?" we will never find happiness. We have in us an urge to know and to grow. Part of this is curiosity. Part is a search for contentment. Ultimately we are searching for wholeness. No matter our outer circumstances, throughout our lives we never feel complete. This incompleteness is uneasy at best, intolerable at worst.

We are incomplete because we are not connected to the transcendent or transpersonal dimensions of our experience. In Indonesian Islamic mystical tradition there is the notion of *Nafsu*. These are the forces, passions and energies that tempt us, seduce us and divert us from recognizing our true humanity. However there is a sublime Nafsu, given to humans for their ultimate blessing—the Nafsu of desire for spiritual realization. This is still a craving, part of our lower nature, but it pushes us in the right direction—toward God. Even in our limited state we always feel an urge toward something more meaningful, more complete and whole.

Approaching this Book

We are in this world to experience life as fully and deeply as possible, in all its many dimensions. Through experience we expand and grow into ourselves, become more completely who we are. Nothing is irrelevant; no part of our being can be neglected or denied. This is the theme of the book.

The first section, Part I, explores the nature of experience, its processes and dimensions. It offers a new way of seeing ourselves using the mirrors of *process, flow, connection and wholeness*. Part II, applies these notions to the question, "How do we become who we are?" We look at those aspects of life that help or hinder, create or restrict our ability to experience more fully. The last section, Part III, sets out what I believe are the bare essentials for living a whole life.

This is the skeleton of the book—not its soul. Because the writing is about experience, it contains many examples from my own and my client's lives. I do not try to make it nice and simple; that is not how real lives are. In our search for what is most valuable in being human, we must embrace all the perplexity and complexity of life. Then we find something beyond our conscious expectations.

Think of this work as a *dreaming* of what it is to understand human nature. Sometimes a dream has startling clarity and we immediately grasp its meaning. At other times it slips through the fingers of our mind. The word "dream" evokes a far simpler idea than the reality of our intense night-time experiences with their essential intangibility and mystery. My dreaming is not your dream; at best it is a map suggesting where to look for reality—a finger pointing at the moon, not the moon itself.

I invite you to inhabit my mind for a little while and see through my eyes. It may seem strange and unfamiliar. As a therapist I wander through the 'in-between' world of experience, struggle with shades of long forgotten memories and navigate tidal waves of crises. I work with intangibles—nothing to get my hands on, no certain results.

If you accept this invitation, you too must let go of certainty and allow your ordinary view of reality to be disturbed. Our efforts to truly understand stir up something deep within us. We know this stirring when we become unsettled; there is something rumbling down there beneath normal awareness. It is as if the neighbors in the apartment below are moving all their furniture. Everything is being rearranged.

I ask you to embrace a different way of seeing, a way to notice the unusual in the obvious, a counterbalance to our tendency to get lost in the taken-for-granted. I ask you to open doors to the unexpected and enter the many rooms in the house of your experience.

A classic hypnotic exercise explores these rooms. The client is asked to relax and drift into a different mode of awareness, to allow the image of a staircase to come to mind. The induction continues: "As you walk slowly down this staircase, notice what the stairs look like and feel each step as it leads you downward. You find yourself in a corridor with many doors. Choose a door, notices its color, size, and the shape of its door handle. You are going to open this door. Behind this door is something of great benefit and interest to you, something that you need for your life. Feel your hand on the knob, carefully turn it and slowly enter."

Everyone finds something different behind the door—and behind each of the other doors. You can never predict what will be there. It may be a beautiful treasure, a haunting memory or a transformative image. It is not always clear why it is so important —but it is.

PART I

Experience and Process

CHAPTER 1

The Gift of Experience

*The little force or clarity I can collect is infinitesimal before
the actual mystery of existence.*
—Lewis Thompson (from *Mirror to the Light*)

People ask what it is like to be a therapist. They say they cannot imagine being in a room listening to depressing stories hour after hour. When it's put like that, I cannot imagine doing it either. Superficially, therapy may look like a painful conversation between two people. That is not the reality.

Let me try to convey what it is like. As I sit with a client, Thomas, nothing extraordinary seems to be happening, yet so much is going on. The room is warm and the chair comfortable— my back a little stiff from gardening. Glancing around, I notice my favorite pictures and objects, the katalpa tree outside and the foothills of the Rocky Mountains beyond, wisps of morning mist still clinging to the pine trees. The Colorado sky is glorious blue as usual.

My body is still rather slow but there is a surge of energy as I feel a spark of connection between Thomas and myself. A young man in his late twenties, Thomas's dark wiry hair contrasts with his pale and expressive face. He is telling me, in his soft, restrained voice about meeting a woman at work. I can see the excitement in his eyes. This is significant for him yet he carefully reins in his hopefulness, protecting himself from another devastating disappointment.

I notice the ambivalence in his body, a struggle to contain the vitality and enthusiasm that wants to break free. His words flow around me, stimulating not only my thoughts, but also many subtle, indescribable feelings. My heart is touched by his dilemma. It is so richly human, so ordinary, so much an expression of the way he is. Naturally moving into a new fullness, he requires only my undivided attention. I sense the moment with its particular texture and quality and feel a deep sense of satisfaction.

Being a therapist provides a special opportunity to notice experience. It is an essential aspect of the work. But each of us can create a similar opportunity by stopping and being aware of ourselves, here and now in this instant of space and time; we do not have to search far.

Experience is the air we breathe, the water in which we swim. It is obvious, easy to overlook, ordinary—yet mysteries hide within. If you take a moment and contemplate what it is to be alive, are you not awed by the magic of being human? Your experience is detailed and penetrating, compelling and vivid. Look around at what you can see, sense the movement of your feelings, catch one of your fleeting thoughts; the complexity of your being is truly astounding. Experience is a commonplace miracle.

Experience

So what can we say about this miracle? There is one fundamental truth: we only know what we experience and our experience is unique.

You are awake at this moment, so you are aware of things around you. If you fell asleep reading this, your world would not change that much, but it would cease to exist for you. It would not be a part of your conscious experience. We only know those events that impact our experience directly.

If you were colorblind, your perception of objects would be different from mine. Your red might be my green, my blue might be your gray. We would live in slightly different universes. Following that thought, we realize that each of us has a distinctive psychological and neurological make up—so our way of experiencing is also unique.[1]

If you have siblings you can test whether this is true. Ask them about some shared family event in your childhood—a vacation, a crisis or a special holiday. There will be some points of agreement but many differences. I know that when my sister tells me of her early life, I am amazed at how unlike it was from mine. Our experiences are so dissimilar we might well have been born into different families.

No two people have the same exact experiences. We each live in somewhat divergent worlds. Visionaries and madmen exist further from the center of socially defined 'reality.' Most of us are more careful to stay close to what is safe and conventional. However much we try to conform and be like others, we cannot help but weave our own meanings from the threads of the universe.

Just think of your experience of this book. How do you come to understand what I am writing? The meaning for you is not in the letters, not in the words or even the string of sentences. You see the black marks on the white paper and somehow, magically, create your own sense of what they say. *You* generate the meaning of this book as you read; my written words are catalysts for your understanding.

You cannot argue with experience. Try persuading someone who is afraid of flying that it is enjoyable to be in a plane—or someone who is depressed that life is worth living. No one can legitimately discount or disprove what you see and feel. No one can know what it is to be you or me, so no one can judge the essential truth of our experience.

Let me provide an illustration. A correct and capable woman in her late fifties came to me with an unusual request. For many years Mary had felt panicky—she was afraid of going outside and had odd thoughts about being different. Recently, intimations of abductions by aliens had come unbidden to her thoughts and she wondered if this connected to her fears. She requested hypnosis to investigate what, if anything, may have happened to her.

I gave my usual explanation: *Hypnosis provides no confirmation of the 'truth' of an experience. It simply accesses what is hidden or unavailable to our conscious mind.* She accepted the ambiguity and we embarked on a strange and fascinating journey exploring many 'memories' of alien abductions.

Mary came to therapy sporadically over a few years as each new abduction presented itself, usually through a dream. The hypnotic sessions were taped so she could review what she said in trance. Eventually we seemed to exhaust all traumatic incidents, starting at age three and continuing about every five to ten years up to the recent past. It was like chronicling an alien longitudinal study with regular interventions to see how the human subject progressed. Although we did little traditional psychotherapy, her symptoms cleared up.

Yet we were left with the question, was it all real or not? Did these events actually happen to Mary or were they figments of her imagination? She struggled with this question in great depth and with thoughtful integrity, yet found no definite answers. Her hypnotic recall of events and panic reactions were similar to clients who remember 'normal' traumatic memories. Her pattern of recovery was typical of recovery from abuse. But from the viewpoint of conventional thinking, her experiences were crazy and impossible.

I learned that resolving the question, "Real or unreal?" is not always appropriate or possible. Our cultural obsession with 'the facts' of a situation reflects a deep insecurity with not knowing — a need for certainty and control that cannot ever be fulfilled. More important from the human perspective is to consider, "What is the experience and what does it mean for this person?" Experience exists as a reality and a truth of its own, in its own space, between the physical and imaginal worlds. It is neither material fact nor fictional fantasy; it is something else.

Our deeper experiences constantly tread that line between the real and the unreal. Consider a common dream: *You are running away from a scary person who is going to harm you. Your legs won't move properly, as if they are stuck in quicksand. Your heart is pounding and you can't get a deep enough breath. You wake terrified.* Is this a real experience or not? Your body responds as if you are under deadly threat. The residue of the dream lasts most of the day, making you jumpy and distracted. Your physiological system knows that it is genuine, even if your conscious mind discards it as 'only a dream.' Experiences are always 'real', even when they do not accord with outer happenings.

Out of experiences we build our individuality. Who I am and how I respond to the world, to myself and to other people, is a reflection of all that has gone before. I encounter the world, I know myself and create my personal universe using the bricks and mortar of my experience. If the foundation is sound, the building stands solid; if the materials are questionable, instability results. Experience is all I have and all I know.

Experience is Everything that Affects Us

As I write about experience you might easily find yourself getting lost in the abstract ideas. Experience is hard to grasp because it is not a thing, not a physical event. It exists 'in between'—in the relationship between your self and whatever is affecting you. In that mysterious dimension, a difference emerges that changes you. Every moment a million different forces impinge on you, some you notice, others are more cryptic—but all subtly influence who you are. This is the nature of experience.

In conversation we use the word "experience" to describe an event that is important or impactful—"It was a wonderful experience." We talk about experience as those things we know, feel and recall. Yet this is a partial truth; it only highlights what is available to our consciousness.

Experience is much more than that. If I ask you to notice the feeling in your feet, you become aware of some unrecognized sensation that was there all the time. By shifting your attention you expand your experience to include what is happening in your body. We unconsciously filter our experiences, neglecting most of what is possible to feel, think, or sense at any moment. But it all still exists somewhere, waiting for the breath of awareness to bring it alive.

Every unnoticed sensation or forgotten dream, each fleeting thought or inarticulate feeling, is part of who you are. Your experience includes hopes, fears, aspirations and distractions. It is everything and anything that impacts somewhere, in some form, on your being. You may not feel the impact of background radiation on your bodily cells, the unconscious fantasies in the depths of your psyche; yet those too are part of your experience. You *are* the totality of what you experience in this moment in time, and all moments past. You *will be* the totality of all your life experiences—past, present and future.

My session with Thomas is rich with experience. I hear his words, sense what he is trying to convey and feel his presence. I see how his body shifts with every different thought and emotion that moves through him. Our experiences resonate together as we share laughter, poignancy or touch the mystery of being. All these impressions create my conscious experience.

More subtly, the light changing in the room as the day progresses, the emptiness in my stomach, the tick of the clock—these register somewhere less accessible. I know how much time has gone by and when the session is about to end without having to think. Tiny differences are added up, put together into a sense of implicit knowing.[2] At every moment my living experience is created out of infinite bits of information, some conscious but the majority hidden iceberg-like beneath the surface of awareness.

So why is this important? Because if we only know what we experience and each of us experiences differently, then 'reality' is not fixed. It is a compromise between what is out there and our experience of it. Somehow we co-create the world through shared experiencing, each person adding a piece of individuality, a different brush stroke to the final picture. We are not passive victims of 'reality'—we actively invite and influence the meaning of what happens to us.

Experience is Mutable

We are made of experience and yet we create our experience. That is the paradox. All experience nourishes our humanity — even the darkest. Life necessarily includes disasters, traumas and cruelty and those events we wish to avoid. Yet we are not completely at the mercy of external incidents. These may intrude on us beyond our control, but we ultimately determine the quality of our experience of them.

I have seen many people with devastating chronic pain. Some I can help. One woman, Kathy, stays vividly in my memory mostly because I could make little impact on her debilitating fibromyalgia. Every day and most of her sleepless nights, her neck, shoulders and right arm were tortured with an incessant pulling and twisting agony. The pain was constant, regardless of medication and intrusive medical procedures.

Yet our work together was successful. Through her dreams and inner work she was able to find a place of meaning and quiet acceptance of suffering that allowed her to rise above her disability. Her affliction became a sacred burden, a companion on her life path. With change of attitude came change of experience.

No longer miserable and desperate, she was able to get on with life. The pain remained—but Kathy changed around it.

Experience is the imprint of the universe on our souls. Not passive recipients but active participants, we create the meaning of that imprint. Experience is never immutable; it is not given to us by the world as an inalterable lump. We always have some part to play in how we respond.

This means that you too can change the quality of your experience, although that is not always easy. It takes awareness and effort, and sometimes we need the help of others. The worst trap is to think that we have no influence over who we are, that we cannot change. That way despair lies.

Experience and Process

People come to therapy to change the quality of their experience. Unlike the policeman, lawyer or doctor, a therapist has no direct power over what happens outside of the office. I cannot alter the hassles, losses or tumult of living. What I do is influence the way a person makes sense of his or her experience as it shifts and flows. When we realize that the essence of experience is change, then anything becomes possible.

One of my therapeutic 'homework' assignments is to suggest that a client does one thing different that week. She might respond differently to her partner, think a creative thought or take a different route to and from work. It does not matter what the activity is, and it is best if she does not think about it until the moment arrives—no preparation, no forethought. The intention is to notice the quality of what happens, to approach life from a slightly different angle and thus be moved by the fresh happening.

Each person experiences uniquely. My task is to understand that uniqueness. I ask myself: "Why does this person feel, think and act in this particular way? What is wrong with the way this person approaches their life? What needs to happen so he or she can experience more fully?" To understand these questions I have to make sense of something more fundamental: What is the nature of experience?

Possibly this is an unanswerable question. Yet some aspects of it are self-evident. Experience moves in an ever-changing flow from the past, through the present, into some potential future. Each experience in every moment is different from every other. There may be similarities and predictable patterns that create our shared knowledge of the world, but we can never recapture what has passed.

If you read that last sentence again, even though it does not seem to have changed in itself, your understanding, your experience of it, will have subtly shifted from the first time. You are not precisely who you were even a second ago. You have moved on.

This changing and shifting aspect of experience is called *process*.[3] Process is not the experience itself; it is the flowing movement out of which our experience arises, an infinitely complex and constantly changing stream. Process is the essence of motion, the flux that sustains and creates all we know.[4]

The relationship between experience and process is that between wind and moving air, between the river and flowing water. We feel the wind but cannot see the air from which it arises. We think we know the river yet it is never unchanged from one moment to the next; the water is always in motion. The movement of air and of water creates the perception of wind and river. Just so, the flow of process creates all our experience.

Concern with process is part of a current shift in the way modern researchers understand the world.[5] According to recent theories in physics, the universe is not entirely predictable, not a solid aggregation of mechanical elements that run like clockwork.

Recent scientific explanations have become more complex and subtle, attempting to understand the 'strangeness' of quantum interactions, the way life organizes itself, the 'order of chaos.'[6] We are asked to accept that the universe, and everything in it, is a vast interconnected whole of which we are some small part.[7] All we know exists within a graceful web of interconnectedness. If one strand is touched, the whole web vibrates in sympathy, some parts more and some parts less.

Our human experience is part of that web and shares a similar essence. Small shifts in the way we think or feel ripple through our being. Subtle variations in our environment profoundly affect our state. We are not fixed or changeless objects; we are beings of flowing experience. That flow is the movement of innumerable processes in motion throughout our being.

The Gift of Experience

From the moment of conception we respond to the universe. Growing up, we gain a measure of choice in that response. Some choose to remain passive recipients of whatever comes their way. They feel at the mercy of the world—and this becomes increasingly true. What happens to them, and how they react, become welded into one, inseparable, unchangeable lump. Not choosing the quality of their experience, they react more and more habitually to whatever happens. They leave no space for choice.

I once saw a wealthy man, Jason, for a few sessions. With all the resources at his disposal, with no need to ever work, he still constantly rushed around, unable to be still. During therapy his cell phone would ring and he would automatically answer; there was no space for his inner life. Educated and intelligent, his mind knew what he needed to do to change, yet he couldn't or wouldn't do it. We did not get far in therapy before he was off onto the next distraction.

To live authentically—to be the most we can be—is a formidable task. It requires more than an intellectual understanding, more than a wishing or hoping. We cannot do it without awareness, without an unshakable intention to notice, engage and choose our experience. Each and every moment is a test of that intention. It demands we ask of ourselves, "Am I as fully in this experience as I can be?"

Ask yourself that question now. Does the world around you look vibrant? Can you sense your own vitality flowing through your being? When you are in your experience you are fully alive. When you fail to rise to that challenge, you feel dense and solid, a hazy cloud dulling awareness and splitting you from yourself. It may feel 'normal' but you can sense something essential is missing.

Experience is a precious, sacred gift. It is given to us free and clear with no strings attached. We can do with it what we will. When we are engaged with life, experience evolves. But unlike natural selection, we are intimately concerned with that evolution. Our choices influence how, as well as what, we experience. Entering a room full of strangers, I can decide to be myself, be friendly, enjoy meeting these new people—or I can put on a false front, be aloof and stand-offish. The choice is mine and the resulting experience is mine.

To experience more we have to become more—more present, more aware and more connected. As the ability to experience grows, so does our responsibility; we implicitly agree to embody a wider vision of what it is to be human. No longer is it enough to think only of ourselves, distinct from all else. We begin to see and feel the interconnectedness of everything—to become whole. Becoming whole we begin to tread the path of holiness.

CHAPTER 2

Process: The Flow of Life

And a voice came to me, saying:
In every creature, in forest and ocean, in leaf and tree and
bird and beast and man, there moves a spirit other than its
mortal own,
Pure, fluid, as air—intense as fire,...
—Edward Carpenter (from *Among the Ferns*)

Moving is natural, stagnation is sickness.
—Attributed to Lao Tzu

I am sitting at the open door of my hogan, an eight-sided wooden cabin built into the steep mountainside. It is a quiet place for writing and contemplation. The doorway looks out over the pine-clad foothills of the Rockies to a straight-line horizon fifty miles away on the plains. Sun shines from the deep blue sky. I hear birds and the wind restlessly moving the branches.

A gnarled ponderosa pine sweeps over the hogan. It holds onto life despite lightening strike, insect boring and old age. I notice the resin oozing from its flaky reddish bark, the twisted limbs connecting to twigs and bunches of pine needles. It is like a Chinese painting in its hoary perfection.

No disorder intrudes on this scene. Everything—trees, grasses,

35

rocks, dirt, pine needles and broken twigs—is meant to be here. Everything has its place, its way of being, its part to play in an ever-changing wholeness. This ponderosa pine is unique, completely itself. I can sense its aliveness as it slowly grows and changes through the seasons. It is a living system, intimately connected to earth, sun, air and moisture—part of the surrounding forest, one among many trees in this whole mountain ecology.

My seeing and appreciation is also part of another whole. As I look and connect, I am linked to everything for these moments. My experience of this tree and my awareness of that experience create something new that begins to extend into this description. You read these words; a further transformation occurs. Now you are part of this description—this is your experience of my seeing. Your experience joins with mine and so the ripple expands another circle out into the universe.

Experience is never still; it has to be in motion. As Lao Tzu says, movement is alive, inertia is dead. This is most true of our being. We are fully alive only when we are immersed in the flow of living experience; we become more 'un-alive' as we cling to that which is predictable and unchanging.

Look around you. What do you notice? Probably you see the things and objects that make up your immediate environment: this book, the furniture, walls, floor and windows. Everything looks normal, solid and real. It feels tangible and substantial when you touch it. There is something unexceptional and predictable about this material world. It stays put. It has "object constancy." You can rely on things to be there, essentially the same, if you leave them and come back later.[1]

You have read or heard in school that material things are mostly made up of minutely tiny bits of energy/matter whirling in vast amounts of space. You may even have been told that those infinitesimal bits do not really exist in a way that we can understand. But this knowledge has little impact on your concrete experience here and now. It is all interesting in theory, but it is not really 'real.'

But take a step backward into yourself. Notice your body and changing sensations. How are your hands feeling? Is your breathing easy? Are you relaxed or restless—what small movements are happening without you willing them? Your body is also a material thing but it does not seem quite so constant as the objects around you. It keeps changing moment to moment—and you feel those changes as shifts in your experience.

Again, academic knowledge tells you that your body is an amazingly complex collection of limbs and organs—blood, bone and tissue—neurons, cells and biochemical reactions. It is always in motion—but you forget unless it signals that it is thirsty, tired, in pain or unsettled. Then for a while you remember that it is not really a *thing*. It is *you*, and it keeps demanding attention—getting older, growing hair, needing to go to the bathroom, fidgeting and breathing. It is never, for a single moment, completely static, even when you sleep. Your body is like those bits of energy whirling in space; while alive, it never stops moving and changing.

Look inwards a little deeper. Notice your feelings and fleeting associations. You may be able to hold a single image or idea in your mind for a few seconds with effort, but then it moves and transforms. If you relax a bit and stay aware, you can notice your "stream of consciousness"—a never ending train of thoughts, feelings and fantasies emerging from the back of your mind.[2] You grasp at a thought that is in motion. It slips away and becomes something else. There is no 'thing' to touch and hold.

This is the ultimate demonstration. Your mind, your awareness —the means through which you experience the world as solid and stable—are utterly shifting and flowing. The deeper we explore outer and inner reality, the more we find that everything is insubstantial, in process of movement and change. Our ordinary perceptions of a solid and stable universe are mostly illusion. In fact, all around us and within us is a vast flux, constantly evolving and shifting. It is a living motion picture, ever changing—moving inexorably from the past into the future. Yet we constantly freeze this movie into a series of still photographs.

Now we find the dilemma. Our mind, with its perceptions and ideas, is designed to highlight all that is most predictable and relevant for survival. It creates the experience of a solid and reliable world. But in doing so it masks the truth.[3] We are fully convinced that things are constant. Yet even as we finish this sentence, everything is different from when we started—atoms whirling, mind shifting, galaxies journeying through space—the universe has moved on. This is the predicament: do we assume the accuracy of our taken-for-granted perceptions, or do we dig deeper into a different, more fluid way of knowing?

Each perception is an edited and abstracted version of whatever is out there. Ordinary convictions and 'common sense' assumptions are part of what blinds us. When we look inward at the texture of experience—flowing, shifting, ever moving—we begin to get a clearer grasp of what is most essential. That is *change* itself.

We cannot gaze at this shifting scenery too long. We look away from the dizzying movement toward something solid to soothe the disorientation it provokes. Like children spinning on a merry-go-round, we desperately fix our eyes on the ground so as not to lose balance. It is hard to accept that our humanness, and maybe all we can know, is made of *movement* and not of stuff that stands still.

To understand our experience, we have to capture this movement. If we can only ensnare that fleeting intuition of motion, then we conceive of ourselves in a profoundly different way. We look deeper into the mystery of experience and know that we are transient beings on a journey of becoming. We are always proceeding to some unknown and unpredictable future; we are not things—we are *process*.[4]

What is Process?

I remember being fascinated and disturbed as a child that saying the same word over and over drained it of all semblance of meaning and that staring fixedly at a point caused everything to flow in a weird, unrecognizable way. It made me wonder what was real or unreal. My adolescent experiments with hallucinogens helped me realize that the solidity and familiarity of the world is only paper thin. Beneath the surface everything we hold true is called into question.

Throughout history great thinkers have been intrigued with similar questions about the nature of reality. How can everything be changing and yet seem to remain the same? Is anything ever constant? Is our experience of the world and ourselves real, or is it an illusion? These are profound and difficult enigmas that science, philosophy and religion have tried to address in different ways. Out of this vast accumulation of ideas, I will touch on a small sample to provide us with some useful landmarks.

Ancient Wisdom

In Western tradition it was Heraclitus, a Greek philosopher of the fifth century BC, who first proposed that everything is flux and change. Heraclitus is credited with the saying that, "you can never step twice into the same river."[5] His words come down to us in pithy epigrams that are somewhat obscure but embody a profound wisdom.

"All things come into being through opposition, and all are in flux, like a river."[6] This fragment suggests that the universe is in a constant state of change characterized by a ceaselessly shifting conflict of opposites.[7] Driving this change is a creative energetic essence that Heraclitus likened to, "an everlasting fire, kindling by measure and going out by measure."[8]

Later Greek philosophers called this energy for change, *Physis* or Life Force, a useful shorthand to describe the mysterious workings of the creative process that imbues everything with a dynamic energy.[9] In humans, the Life Force is the vital living essence of all our processes, the spark in our experience.

When we look to the East we find similar wisdom in ancient China. The *I Ching* or "Book of Change", one of mankind's oldest texts, is first and foremost a guide to the workings of process. It tells us that change itself, unfolding in time, is the most essential aspect of the universe, particularly in the development of the individual soul.[10] For over 3000 years the *I Ching* has been treated with the utmost reverence both as a philosophical text and as a practical means of divination:

> It (the *I Ching*) has the omniscience of a Buddha. It speaks to the transient world as though from the Womb of Change itself—Change, the one constant factor amidst all the countless permutations and transformations of mental and material objects which, when the eye of wisdom is closed, appears to us as a meaningless flux.[11]

Like Heraclitus, the *I Ching* proposes that all things arise and change in patterns of opposites, those of *receptive* Yin and *active* Yang.[12] The universal indivisible principle encompassing both Yin and Yang in Chinese thought is named *Tao*. Tao is the *Way* of the universe, its indescribable primordial nature. Tao is unknowable in itself and can only be glimpsed enigmatically through our experience of changing creation.

About 600 BC, a profound text, the *Tao Teh Ching*, was written down, possibly by a sage called Lao Tzu. Its terse epigrammatic style (somewhat similar to Heraclitus) attempts to capture the essence of Tao. There are countless translations of the *Tao Teh Ching*, none of which agree exactly. I have chosen a translation of verse twenty one that I feel expresses the mysterious fluid nature of Tao:

> Tao, as the absolute Truth of the universe, is elusive and

evasive.

Though it is elusive and evasive, it unveils itself as images and forms.

Evasive and elusive, it discloses itself as indefinable substance.

Shadowy and indistinct, it reveals itself as impalpable subtle essence.

This essence is so subtle and yet so real.

It is the primary origin of the whole of creation.[13]

Tao is the indefinable dynamic principle behind all creation. Everything we know reflects this principle, which fills all creation with life and vitality. Tao manifests in the things that we can touch see and feel with our senses; it moves through us in the ever-changing, flowing energetic pattern of our experience. Yet we can never grasp it fully with our minds.

Ancient Greek and Chinese thinking seem to agree: the universe comes into existence through a transcendent force that permeates all creation, flowing in accord with a fundamental principle of constant change. When we are in harmony with the way the universe itself moves, our being flows naturally toward a state of wholeness.

A Modern Viewpoint

This all might seem rather obscure and esoteric, and certainly unscientific. Yet as we shift perspective from the ancient East to the modern West, we find a surprising agreement. David Bohm, a profound theoretical physicist, conceptualizes the whole universe as manifestation of the *universal flux*, almost another name for Tao.

(The universal flux) can perhaps best be called *Undivided Wholeness in Flowing Movement*. This view implies that flow is, in some sense prior to that of the 'things' that can be seen to form and dissolve in this flow.

One can perhaps illustrate what is meant here by considering the 'stream of consciousness.' This flux of awareness is not precisely definable, and yet it is evidently prior to the definable forms of thoughts and ideas which can be seen to form and dissolve in the flux, like ripples, waves and vortices in a flowing stream.[14]

Bohm tells us that everything *is* process; everything is *in* process.[15] What this means is that nothing is constant, nothing can exist beyond the principle of change. There are no stable, enduring phenomena anywhere in the universe.

The Illusion of Stability

The idea of process is hard to grasp and harder to translate into a convincing experience. Why, if all is change, do we experience the world as relatively stable? How do we derive a false idea of permanence from the passing impressions that touch our senses? Maybe like the TV or movies, our eyes ignore the flicker of thousands of different images to produce a constant picture that makes sense.

Occasionally, in different states of awareness when the conscious mind is bypassed, we can experience more closely, the way the universe really is. Aldous Huxley, reflecting on his experiences of taking the drug mescaline, suggests that the function of the brain and the nervous system is largely *eliminative*. We cannot usually experience reality in the raw:

> To make biological survival possible, Mind at Large has to be funneled through the reducing valve of the brain and nervous system. What comes out at the other end is a measly trickle of the kind of consciousness which will help us stay alive on the surface of this particular planet.[16]

Our nervous system is not only a "reducing valve" but it is also limited by the particular rate at which it processes information. We perceive objects as solid and stable because, in actuality, they are slower processes than that of the human system. We see them as static because we move faster. The chair you sit in, your physical body, your mind and awareness, each is a manifestation of the universal flux. Each has its own rhythmic vibratory rate, its own velocity. Faster processes are more ephemeral, slower ones apparently more substantial and permanent. Our perception of constancy is an illusion created by *relative velocity*.

I wonder how I appear to the ponderosa pine near my hogan. It probably includes me with those other phenomena such as wind or rain that are fleeting and intangible. I am a phantom to it. In relation to the life and pace of that ancient tree, I move far too fast to be noticeable.

At the opposite end are the glimmering hummingbirds at my feeder, their wings a blur of energy. They ignore me as I come close because I move so slowly in comparison to their pace. The hummingbird flits at lightning speed around me, at least ten times my velocity. To that tiny winged being I appear a sluggish thing, almost tree-like in my movements.

Are there other beings whose speed is so swift that I am a rock to them and they are less than a breeze to me? How would I know? Can I even guess at the being of Gaia, the spirit of this planet, whose single thought might be a thousand years long? I am captured within a tiny range of possible experiences, limited by my neurons.

We do not see the swirl of atoms or the hectic race of galaxies. Our velocity and sensory apparatus limit us. We imagine the world, and ourselves in it, to be semi-static, filled with enduring objects—things rather than living processes. Yet the truth is more fluid and far more complex, filled with unimaginable possibilities. We are ripples in a vast flowing ocean of universal movement.

The Shape of Process

Most people love to walk along a beach, watching and hearing the ocean waves rolling rhythmically onto the sand. Why is this sound and motion so potent, so absorbing? There is an archetypal aspect to the movement of waves that touches a deep knowing within us. Waves are a living reminder of the shape of our lives and experience: the movement of fluid energy rises up, rolls along and breaks apart into a calming wash—ever-changing, powerful yet ephemeral. This is the profile of each and every process.

Process has a consistent design, a wave-like pattern: arising, continuing, and transforming. Everything—except perhaps the universal flux, Tao, God—comes into being, is embodied or differentiated for a period of time, and then dissolves or transmutes into a different form.[17] This is the cycle of birth, life, and death—the beginning, middle and end that defines every phenomenon.

Process is mysterious, ungraspable, because it has only this one dimension—*duration*. It is not made of anything; it has no depth, height or breadth. It is a movement that exists only in time, not in space. Yet it does have impact; we know it through its effect. We don't see the wind, but we see and hear the leaves rustling.

Like an ocean wave, process is a moving flow of energy that creates the deceptive perception of water in motion. Even though that roller does not actually propel the water toward you, it can knock you down, engulf you. Its power is not illusory. Particular processes are ripples, rollers, tsunamis in the ocean of the universal flux; each has its own quality and imprint. Can you imagine yourself and all around you as waves breaking against some mysterious shore?

Some of these waves are immeasurably long. The formation of stars, the spinning of our spiral galaxy, the expansion of the universe since the Big Bang—these take eons to unfold. In comparison, the total span of human existence is a brief instant. At the opposite end of the scale, subatomic particles oscillate at a rate almost beyond the ability of time to measure. They exist at the extreme edge of manifestation, almost, but not quite coming into being as we know it.

Within this vast range, everything has its own rhythmic frequency, its surging pattern. Living beings take the middle ground. Life, as we recognize it, exists in a narrow range of frequencies. Here we find those processes that define what it is to be human—the pattern of being born, living, experiencing and dying that circumscribe our nature.

Within a human being each life process has its own span. Our neurons are stimulated, fire off a series of signals and then rest. We are hungry, we eat and then stop eating; we are tired, we sleep and then wake; we feel aroused, become sexual, reach orgasm and relax. You can only read this book for so long before you need a break to do something else. Every experience, every feeling, has its beginning, its duration and then its end or transformation.

I learned this directly, working with grief and bereavement when I visited a young mother in her home. Her husband had died slowly of a horrible neurological disorder a month previously. She was totally distraught, weeping uncontrollably as we talked about him. She told me she would never get over his loss, never move his bed from the living room or his cigarettes and lighter from the ashtray. I began to wonder if she would cry forever.

Emphatic as she was, her sobbing began to ease after about forty minutes. I learned that no matter how painful a feeling, most people can only cry for just so long. Within three months, she had cleared out her husband's things, except for a few precious momentos. She became engaged with life at around six months, and after just over a year, she was exploring new friendships. Her grieving process progressed naturally, each aspect having its own particular pace and duration.

Unless a process is stuck, it will progress toward its natural conclusion. Each period of waking is just so long before we sleep. Each night dream lasts an average of twenty minutes. Each thought (unless we are obsessing) naturally proceeds into another. That all experience is finite is one of the blessings and also disappointments of living. Pain ends, but so does joy. If we simply allow each process to have its term, get out of the way of the flow, the movement toward wholeness will take us on a new path. That path is the journey of life.

Process and Life

It is astonishing how many different meanings there are to the word *life*. 'Life' is all living beings and it is also my experience of being alive. It is the active principle that sustains vitality and it is the whole span of my being in this body. Can I really separate these meanings? My personal life is part of the greater life. To be alive is to know life.

As much as we are alive, life remains one of those sacred mysteries. Within a material universe that seems to move inexorably toward entropy—disorder, disintegration, sameness— living beings struggle against the torrent. The Life Force is *negentropic*—differentiating, organizing, integrating and creating more of itself.[18]

Look at the incredible variety of living organisms on this earth and the impossibly precise way in which these organisms connect together to create evolving ecologies. Interconnection and symbiosis are the rule rather than the exception. In our guts are bacteria and enzymes essential for digestion—in our beds are dust mites consuming our discarded skin cells. Life fills every available niche from the volcanic vents on the ocean floor to the coldest wastes of Antartica. As an organism evolves, it binds to other life forms, creating new complex partnerships and increasing its probability of survival. The more connected to the whole, the more likely it is to endure and develop.

Life acts as if it has a purpose, as if it knows which direction to take. It seems to seek out, or is attracted toward, some ultimate end point that is more whole and complete.[19] In the introduction we recognized this as the "actualizing and formative tendency" that sets the direction for our growth. Traditional biologists call it

46

evolution and assume that it is driven by random mutation and 'survival of the fittest.' However, when we examine experience, we find that deterministic ideas of simple cause and effect cannot capture its complexity.[20] Living organisms are not ultimately predictable.[21]

To be alive is to be involved in a process of growth and increasing connection. Look at your own life. Think about all the things you have learned—all the essential abilities that you take for granted, like talking, reading or driving a car. Remember how you were as a child, or even as an adult a few years ago and notice how you keep changing and developing. Life does not stand still; it evolves constantly, connecting and reconnecting. The universe is involved in a process of becoming increasingly alive, and we are part of that enlivening.[22]

We each have our own unique life process that gives us the experiences, the raw materials out of which we create ourselves. Once, a client asked me if I had a good life. Somewhat taken aback, and slightly wary that this might be a subtle 'trap', I took some time to think it over. Eventually, I decided to share the truth of my experience: I said I had a wonderful life, very full and satisfying.

I asked why she wanted to know. Her reply was interesting. Almost all her life had been horrible, full of fear and distress. She wanted to know that there were other possibilities to experience. I inquired if she wished for my life instead of her own. Very emphatically, she said, "No. I may hate my life but it is mine; it belongs to me alone. I wouldn't be me if I had a different life." Each life defines who we are. It is woven into the fabric of our being, given to us as a task and a unique winding path toward realization of ourselves.

The River of Life

Let's create a dream-like image of the life process. Picture a river you know. As you sit on its banks the river is always changing, flowing onward. Within the river's flow, you see the droplets of water, the waves and swirls, the depths and surface, the motion and stillness. Every part goes to make up that particular river: the water channeled between the changing riverbanks, the contoured rocky bottom, the silent pools and turbulent rapids. The river has direction—gravity pulling constantly toward a final merging with the ocean.

This river is a metaphor for your whole life. The flowing water is both your life essence and the movement of your experience. You begin as a tiny spring bubbling up at your conception. Your life ends, joining with the ocean, at your death. In the upper reaches it runs vigorously, a small stream cutting a channel into the mountainside; this is your childhood.

As the stream gathers substance on its journey, it becomes the turbulent creek of adolescence, tumbling and churning, furrowing deeply into bedrock. It reaches the flatter lands of adulthood, increasing in power and begins to spread into a more sedate well-worn form. Sometimes the flow is muddied, foaming and tempestuous as it moves through narrow rapids; other times it meanders leisurely and sluggish, twisting and turning around obstructions. Finally, replete with life, the river merges with the seawater at its estuary. Now the essence has transformed; the watery elements have become ocean.

Your life process is the complete river from beginning to end. You are the flowing totality, not any single element. Who you think you are, your consciousness, travels as a wave on the surface of the water, from near the beginning all the way to the end. That is the small self, the ego caught in time, acting as witness to the journey. That small wave cannot recognize the whole, does not know the depths and profound complexity of it all.

From one single viewpoint we cannot see the spread of the river from its trickling source to its sea delta. We cannot capture the river, cannot hold the fluidly changing form of our life. Only slices of reality are available to our limited awareness.

The river metaphor, lifted from Heraclitus, portrays the process of living experience. We are immersed in dynamic 'watery' elements—flowing, swirling in strange, chaotic motions. Always we are moving in some direction we cannot wholly know. Yet somehow we are able to influence our journey, decide to some extent where and how we travel. The final path, its speed and motion, is a covenant between our intentions and the way life moves us.

Tuning to the Life Force

Life has been transmitted from one living being to another in an unbroken line stretching back to the dawn of time. We are the recipients of a priceless gift that demands an innovative response. Looking deeply into the universe and our beings, we discover a luminous insight: life, and our experience of it, is a profound flowing, mutable process.

Processes are waves on the surface of the universal flux. Your being is a particular waveform. It comes into existence, continues for a period and then subsides; this is your birth, your life and your dying. Change cannot be avoided—risk and difficulties are inevitable. You are being swept along on the river of your life.

How should we respond to this realization? Even with millennia of religious practices, even with shelves of psychology self-help books, we are still at a loss. The fact is each process and each path is unique. There are no schedules, no precise recipes for living and growing. I cannot tell you exactly what you should do— neither can any authority, whether therapist or guru. We each must find our own way, a way that resonates with the nature of our individuality.

To know ourselves we begin to sense the flow of our own process, feel it in our bones, our hearts and our minds. Moving through life, we recognize and appreciate our own small wave, part of the whole. There is a quality of ease, of rightness, as we move with the flow of the Life Force—with Tao, the Way of life. We are in tune with the transcendent.[23]

Sensing the undercurrents, it becomes easier to recognize the eddies and obstructions that create turbulence. Maybe we can elude them; maybe we can move through them more fluidly—but more importantly, can we recognize the true direction and purpose of our life journey?

Bapak Muhammad Subuh Sumohadiwidjojo, a wise spiritual guide, tells us that one night while praying he received a large book filled with living, moving pictures. Each page showed him illustrations of his life task. He saw people of different colors and races being together, each moving to their own rhythm. As he hugged the book to him it vanished into his chest.[24] This was his 'book of life.'

We too must find the flowing words and pictures that are written on our soul. The Life Force demands that we experience fully, that we neglect nothing, that we resonate with the movement of the universe. Then we are truly *living in process*.

CHAPTER 3

The Dimensions of Process

I am deeply convinced that the transcendent is present in human life: it allures man and acts in human existence. I have known the depth and power of the sub-conscious and the subterranean, but I have also known the other and greater deep which is transcendence.
—Nikolai Berdyaev

Some years ago, lost in reverie on a long wintry walk among the snow and pines of the mountains, I became immersed in tranquility. The trees were utterly alive and quietly watching—the snow soft and deep, deadening all sound. Crossing a frozen creek, I explored a rocky outcrop that had been trampled by the prints of deer. It was a magical place. I could imagine great bucks, regal against the sky, overlooking their domain. On my slow return, images and insights came to my heightened awareness.

Much is now lost but I retain the central impression: human beings are 'doorways' between different worlds. Experience flows through us like breath, enlivening and enriching, moving in and out. From our outer world the portal opens inward to another life—"A Life Within a Life."[1] From that other world flows meaning, spirit and vitality. Our task as human beings is to become resilient entrances—open to that energetic traffic which creates more life and richness, closed to that which may pollute or harm.

Pondering these images I realize there are many dimensions of *in* and *out*. Every inside is also an outside to somewhere else. Experience extends ever inward, ever outward and into realms where 'in' and 'out' join to create some greater whole. Over time, I have found that dimensions of experience have become more apparent, more transparent. Searching for a simple way to describe the infinite complexity of human processes, I have come to imagine a series of nested levels that extend from the most profound to the mundane.

Sometimes, especially with certain clients, I sense a movement and purpose beyond anything that is spoken or understood—a numinous, transpersonal dimension to our being together. I call this the *Greater process*, the ground of our being.[2] It makes itself known as a quiet, encompassing awareness that something greater than we realize is going on. My first therapist, Winifred Rushforth, would often say with particular emphasis, *"Something is Happening."*[3] She was directing our attention to the presence of the transcendent within every moment.

Out of this encompassing greater movement emerges all that underlies our consciousness—the impersonal, unconscious, symbolic, imaginal aspect of our selves. I call this the *deeper process*, the substratum of who we are. This is always present just below awareness, just at the edge of our peripheral vision, seeping up into the back of our minds.

The deeper process speaks to us in dreams and fantasies, subtle intuitions, spontaneous body movements and altered states of awareness. When we stop for a moment and let our normal self loosen a little, it is waiting to inform us of the bigger picture, the way things need to move and change. This is the fertile loam out of which individuality arises.

The Greater and deeper levels of experiencing are mostly obscured from us in our day to day life. What we are aware of is our subjective self—all those inner experiences that make up our sense of who we are. This I think of as the *inner process*, the basis of the experience of 'selfness.' It includes our self-awareness, the ways we typically think, feel emotion and sense our bodies. The inner process is the domain of insight and emotional release, somatic sensing and connecting together pieces of experience. When we are deeply moved by a piece of music, when we feel strongly about some valued belief, we are in touch with our inner process.

The quality of our inner experience determines, to a great extent, the way we act on and in the world. The *doing* aspect of our experience—not *what* we do, but *how* we do it—I call the *outer process*. When you tell a friend what happened to you during the week, you are describing your outer experience and implicitly expressing your outer process *in the way* you tell the story.

This fourfold model of process is how I understand experience in myself and in others. I imagine the more personal dimensions as wave forms that each emerge out of more encompassing waves. These waves travel upon an ocean that is the Greater process.

The Dimensions of Process

Process in Psychotherapy

Let me describe how I might observe the different levels in a psychotherapy session. Dave always comes a few minutes late to his sessions, rushing in with a cursory apology. He has to drag himself away from his work as a computer engineer; it consumes him. Short, stocky with dark curly hair, he brings his intense East Coast energy to everything he does.

As usual, he begins by relating all the details of his week—the politics at work, difficulties with his girl friend, trouble with his car. He talks fast with a feverish enthusiasm that jumps from topic to topic. It is not easy to follow, but I try to clarify the main issues and events with sporadic questions and comments.

As Dave talks I get a sense of the way he is in the world, his *outer process*. He flits across the surface of his life like a dragonfly, stopping abruptly here and there between bursts of speed. There is a sense of strain to his way of being in the world. Although successful, he cannot settle or let go of control. It is as if he has to stay on the surface to avoid whatever is underneath.

After a while, and with some prompting, he begins to settle down. Out of the morass of information something important presents itself—a doorway inward. His girl friend has threatened to break off their relationship. I notice a softening of his face, a pensive look. His right hand makes small rubbing movements on the arm of the chair. As he tells me he doesn't know how to handle the situation, I sense he is beginning to connect with his *inner process*.

It is not easy for him to stay with the fear of losing her. I have to remind him to "keep feeling" and not jump to his normal strategy of trying to *fix* it. This inner place is unfamiliar territory. His anxiety threatens to overwhelm him.

As we explore previous failed relationships, he begins to recognize that at some level he does not expect women to want to stay with him, he is not worthy of their love. He remembers how depressed he became when his college lover, Jeanie, dumped him for another guy. He could not get to class for weeks.

Now we have found an entryway to a deeper place. I suggest he relax, and in his mind go back to the moment when Jeanie told him it was finished. He moves into a more diffusely unfocused state as he has done before with me. The *deeper process* becomes more evident. As he pushes back in the chair, his eyes close naturally. His responses slow even more, as images drift into his mind from somewhere else. He begins to describe in a low tone what he is experiencing; there are long pauses.

"I am in my room.... Jeanie comes in. She looks tense. There is this weird energy.... She says she is seeing this other person. She wants to be friends.... I can't breathe. I feel as if something has hit me.... I say it's OK.... She leaves and I don't know what to do. I just sit there."

Each word seems dredged up from somewhere deep inside him. His voice is flat but tears trickle slowly from the corners of his eyes. He makes no move to wipe them away. I ask what does that feeling remind him of? An image of his mother comes to mind but he cannot make sense of it. She looks cold and distant. He knows he has done something wrong but he does not know what it is. It is in his childhood house and he has been put in his room for something. It seems like he is alone forever.

We work for a while with the images, finding ways for that little boy to make sense of his imprisonment. I bring him back to his ordinary awareness. He is a little disoriented but begins to piece together some old memories. He tells me how his mother would get distant and disapproving whenever he did anything she did not like. He learned early to be "good" but even that did not always work. He wonders how this all connects to his problems with his girl friend.

I notice that as he talks now, it is much easier to stay in his inner feelings. He seems more settled and thoughtful. The manic energy is subdued. There is a sense of connection between his outer self and other levels of experience. He is feeling more whole. I am satisfied that I have helped him connect and that he has been able to experience himself a little more deeply. I know that his feelings will flow a little more freely in future.

In this session, the *Greater process* was not explicit. I felt it as a quiet guiding presence that allowed the whole session to move forward smoothly. It was there as an underlying impulse toward connection and wholeness.

Later in therapy it became more evident. Dave's dreams began to touch on religious and spiritual themes. In one dream an old dilapidated Gothic church on campus was under renovation. Inside the old shell a new modern structure was being constructed and he was to do the drawings. He felt somewhat of a fraud because he was not a qualified architect, but the drawings were acceptable.

He began to develop his own regular contemplative practice through sitting quietly and long peaceful walks in nature. When therapy finished, work was balanced with his relationship and he occasionally experienced a spiritual presence in his life.

Experiencing Process

The above example shows how I encounter the four dimensions of process in therapy. You may wonder if these are relevant to your own experience. Let's explore how you can begin to recognize these dimensions in your daily life.

As you read these words, you are seeing the book and the string of type on the page. You probably do not distinguish the individual letters because your attention is focused more toward trying to understand what I am saying and what I mean. For a moment, notice how you are thinking—what is going on in the 'front' of your mind? There is usually a flow of clearer thoughts against a background of more vague ones. Can you notice the tone of those thoughts?

At the same time your body is sending you signals, making

small movements with or without your awareness. You turn the page, shift posture, blink your eyes, fiddle with your hair, or tap your foot. Your body is dissipating excess energy, maintaining a level of comfort so you can continue to read without distraction. Notice these little shifts.

You are currently observing experiences that surround the activity of reading. These have a certain quality and flow that are hard to describe. You may or may not have a label for it: "paying attention", "being abstracted" or "engrossed." You may even recognize your typical style of attitudes, habits, and feelings toward activities of this kind.

Much of your style depends on the context—whether you read for pleasure or obligation and where you are now. Are you reading easily or struggling with unfamiliar ideas? Do you sit up straight or lounge; do you eat or drink? If you are like me, you may be reading in the bath. No one else is you, so no one approaches reading quite like you.

The way in which you engage with this activity, at this time, reflects who you are and your own unique *process*. Because it is concerned with doing something, it has an instrumental purpose, observable in the world. This is a sample of your *outer process*. Outer process is the mode, manner, or way we *do* our lives.

Now, suppose you take a break from reading and begin to check in with yourself. How are you feeling? What is your present state? Notice those subtle inner responses just below the surface — the familiar background flow to your way of experiencing. It has a certain feeling tone, a sense of "me-ness" that is part and parcel of who you are.

If I ask you the question, "Who are you?" and you do not jump to obvious answers (age, sex, profession, attributes and abilities), what happens? Maybe you find your mind wandering toward evocative ideas, memories and images that say something about you. Maybe you avoid the question and keep reading.

Sense yourself and those subtle physical signals that tell you, "I am here now, alive in this place." Notice the sensations in your hands, the tension in your neck or the expression on your face. Where is your energy, how does it move? Is it stuck or does it flow smoothly?

Ask yourself, "Why am I reading this stuff? Do I have to finish it? Am I still interested?" Notice the feelings that come up: excitement, irritation, unease, boredom. Remember things you need or want to do: a forgotten errand, a feeling of hunger or thirst, a wish to be outside. Notice yourself noticing them.

Sustaining these particular thoughts, feelings, and sensations is a pattern of association and connection, an implicit way of organizing the content of your inner world. This is the nature of your subjective personal experiencing, the flow of who you are. This patterning of experience is your *inner process*.

With this little experiment, you can catch a glimpse of how your sense of self takes form. Our inner process is so familiar, so 'ordinary', that we tend to not notice it. It is closer to us than our seeing, more encompassing than our mode of knowing. Like the outer process, it has a particular and unique form; it reflects who we *feel* we are. It is the context for our way of being.

If we take the outer and inner processes together, they make up our customary and ordinary sense of who we are in life. The outer constitutes the active, objective aspects of our existence; the inner is the receptive, subjective sense of self. They are closely intertwined; outer events effect who we are, who we are affects what we do. Both depend on another layer of process that is more obscure and impersonal. We'll explore that next.

Now I ask the impossible—to read and not read, simultaneously. Close your eyes and allow yourself to drift inward. As soon as you do that you will lose the written word. It is possible to let your attention become fuzzy and diffuse, your mind wandering in a relaxed reverie. Notice the dream-like quality of your experiences. Odd ideas, old daydreams, float up from the back of your mind as you glide closer to a sleepy state.

Remember drifting off last night or waking this morning. Stay there for a moment. Sensations, images and memories automatically arise, connecting together in a bizarre image or fragmented story. Your body lets go and becomes still. Sensations change—tingly, warm, heavy. Feelings grow more distant and disconnected, or unexpectedly amplified.

If you can witness this letting go of consciousness—a difficult but not impossible task—you notice that everything becomes increasingly fluid and drifting. Diffuse ideas arise, connected by a fantasy logic that makes sense only in an ambiguous or fairy-tale way. Everything is hard to grasp or describe, slipping out of memory like vapor. It is the dreamer of dreams, the territory of symbol, myth, and metaphor. This is your *deeper process*, the unconscious underworld of your experience. It provides infrastructure for all physical, emotional and mental processes. Your awareness of who you are emerges anew each morning from this underworld.

If the deeper process is beneath awareness, the Greater process is the *spirit of awareness*. Exploring the transcendent essence of experience creates paradox. How can we describe that which is indescribable, capture that which is all encompassing?

We are all familiar with and, at the same time, unfamiliar with spirituality; it is the experience inside every experience. Spirit is that which connects and unifies. Too often we assume that spirituality belongs only to saints and enlightened beings. Yet we experience it whenever we contact a sense of oneness.

Most of us can recapture a vivid and profound glimpse of everything flowing in a natural way. We know it in childhood and in those fleeting moments of completion and awe. Sometimes this comes while alone in nature or engrossed in some activity or sport. It may result from some contemplative or meditative practice or arrive unexpectedly through grace.

Rest quietly in your own center of awareness. Even while reading, expand that awareness to the whole of your experience, to your connection with your surroundings and then out into the universe. Sense the unity and participation of all things. There is a brightness and meaningfulness, a lightness of body and soul. At its most profound, we realize a joy of being, a letting go of trivial everyday concerns. This is your experience of the *Greater process*.

You are a manifestation of all these dimensions—outer, inner, deeper, and Greater. Some of these you can know consciously while others are more mysterious. All powerfully influence who you are and how you experience. All are essential aspects of your humanity. Once you recognize both the whole and the parts of your experience—the surface and the depths, the inside and the outside—awareness expands. Knowing process, we begin to know ourselves better.

Knowing Our Own Process

Let me provide a short summary.

Outer process: this belongs to the sphere of instrumental doing and external experience—planning and acting in the world and everyday life. The outer is the most familiar level of our experience, the surface of our self.[4]

Inner process: this is the sphere of feeling, values and motivation. It supports the emotions, reflective thinking, and physical sensations of our inner world. This is the level of our personal or subjective experience, intimately connected with our sense of an inner self.[5]

Deeper process: this is the sphere of symbolic impersonal knowing—dreamlike experiencing at the subliminal and unconscious level. The deeper process underlies consciousness, providing the natural foundation for our physical and psychological integration. It feels 'other' than our normal sense of self.[6]

Greater process: this is the sphere of transpersonal being. It has a quality of wholeness, completeness, and connection with the essence of life. This is what we would call the realm of the spirit, the most profound and meaningful experiences of the greater Self.[7]

Outer, inner, deeper, Greater—these are the bones, the skeleton of a way to understand experience. I use it daily to check in with different aspects of myself, different modes of being. So, if I am busy *doing*, busily rushing around, I try to remember to look inward to find what drives me. The outer process needs **reminding** that it is not always the most essential. When we remember that we are more than what we do, more than what appears on the surface, we begin to be self-aware.

In stressful situations, I feel frustrated that I can't get everything done. Beneath this is the fear of not doing it right, of feeling inadequate. Awareness of these feelings may be enough to shift my state of being. I ask myself, "What do I need right now to feel better?" The answer may be simple and direct, or it may be more subtle and complex. In every case the inner process asks that we pay **attention**. Paying attention is the single most powerful thing we can do to help process unravel and move.

When I pause and let my mind go loose, I begin to feel the vibration in my body. Sensing that flow I notice an *otherness* that is me and not me. It is very soothing to feel aliveness well up from that deep pool of natural energy. This diffuse mode of awareness helps me whenever I cannot grasp something with my mind, when I am trying to understand a dream or connect deeply with someone. Often an unexpected intuition will present itself. But it only does so if I am open, listening with full attention as if to a being full of wisdom. The deeper process answers only to **trust and respect**. The more it is honored, the more it offers.

My intention is to be always aware of the Greater process, but naturally I forget much of the time. My relationship with the transcendent feels very personal, so I call it God—though other names seem to work just as well. Whenever I get quiet inside, whether working, playing or resting, it is there, constantly available.

Trying to will this connection does not work; I have to gently unravel the knot that keeps me tied to the small self. This requires a quality of letting go—but letting go with a purpose. The Greater process makes itself known through *intentional surrender*. The Divine, the transcendent, is waiting for us to expand enough to recognize its presence.

We are beings of many levels, each of which has its own form, rhythm, and purpose. As we tune in to each domain and accept its essence, life flows more easily. Remembering ourselves every day in everything we do is the beginning. Paying attention to our inner needs, noticing what is hindering the feeling of inner movement, this is a second essential. Respecting the depths, the dreams, the intuition—and trusting that we have powerful helping forces within us comes next. Finally, we must surrender, on purpose, to a Greater all encompassing force within the universe that leads us to harmony.

CHAPTER 4

Exploring the Dimensions of Process

Flow down and down in ever
widening rings of being.
—Rumi

He who knows in truth this Spirit and knows nature with
its changing conditions, wherever this man may be he is no
more whirled round by fate.
—Bhagavad Gita

Although our family was not Catholic, each Sunday, between the ages of ten and thirteen I would cycle the two miles into town to attend Mass. The services were long and boring, and hard on the knees, but I would watch the nuns and know that they were experiencing something I could not understand—something I wanted but could not name. I would kneel in church daydreaming of becoming a saint.

Later, in reading spiritual and mystical literature of the world, that daydream transformed into a desire to reach 'enlightenment.'[1] I imagined that, like in a Zen story, one day a sudden burst of illumination would hit me and instantly I would *know everything*. Or maybe, like the Buddha, I would effortlessly sink deep into meditation and merge with the universe.

I look back on my innocent spiritual enthusiasms with a kind of poignant amusement. It is both funny and sad to entertain such grandiose visions. The spiritual path, the journey to become a human being, is so much more complex than I realized.

To be human is to balance many different and conflicting yearnings, needs and visions. The physical demands of the world do not cease because we wish them to go away. We need others to love, or our hearts wither and die. Compulsive urges surge up from some dark place within, reminding us of our brotherhood with animals and all living beings. It is a difficult juggling act to be human with so many forces pulling and pushing at us.

Now I believe that the spiritual journey has only one position, only one level of development—and that is the *beginning*. We are all beginners, all learners of the lesson of what it is to be human. Somehow we have to harmonize all levels of our being to become more fully ourselves and thus more connected with the transcendent.

The Limits of Consciousness

All of us have moments of profound insight scattered throughout our lives. Why is it so hard to hold onto them? What keeps us from remembering the unity of life? At a physical level, our senses, thinking, and egos are designed for bodily survival. They distinguish things that help us stay alive. Our eyes and visual cortex create discrete images with phantom lines around objects, the better to recognize what we need. Words and language slice and dice the world and our experience into useful chunks. Continuity and completeness are not so important for day-to-day life. We give up the whole in order to concentrate on the parts.

In some greater reality everything flows together continuously; each process is intimately connected with all others. Yet my experience has only one limited viewpoint. I only look out of my own eyes, and will never see the back of my head. I cannot be in two places at the same time. I do not know how to be awake and asleep simultaneously. I live in a world of either/or, in which things and events seem somewhat piecemeal.

We cannot totally escape the bounds of our consciousness. Immediate experience contains only those things that grab and hold our attention. Everything else sinks into the background. That is the nature of attention; it eliminates and separates the world into one thing at a time.

If you are engrossed in reading, other needs go on hold. You forget about the rest of your experience. Only if your bladder gets full will you stop to go to the bathroom. If something is bothering you—a physical discomfort, an emotional upset or an unfinished project—you will not be able to concentrate. You can keep only a few pieces of information in your mind at one time—about the same amount as in a telephone number. Awareness and attention are severely limited.

To make matters worse, we suffer from 'state dependent memory.' As we shift between different experiences, our ability to recall becomes tenuous; we forget. Did you ever notice how hard it is to hold onto dreams? It takes less than an instant for an image, vivid only moments ago, to glide effortlessly out of our waking mind. Similarly, drug-induced experiences remain hidden until a similar substance is ingested (have you forgotten what you did when you were drunk?). Working in deep hypnotic trance, clients seldom remember the details of what happened, even when they are intense.

Enclosed as we are in our own restricted awareness we tend not to notice its limitations. The mind is tricky; it dismisses contradictions and fills in the gaps of experience. We take it for granted that we lose keys through forgetfulness. We never notice the 'blind spot' that is a hole in our field of vision. With brain injury, we can lose half of our visual field without noticing; the brain just sketches in the missing part. Our memory of distant events is perhaps 50% accurate—cobbled together from actual details and what probably happened. We delude ourselves if we think that we completely know the nature of our own reality.

Disconnected from Experience

We are not only deluded, we are also disconnected. Like Dave in the last chapter, most of us identify ourselves with outer experience: "I am what I do." This rift between the outer and inner processes makes it impossible to fully experience. How can you make any sense of the inner world if you do not feel it? A reliance on outer activity helps avoid unpleasant inner feelings. It is easier to get on with life if we don't have to bother with the messiness of emotions, yearnings and imagination, but then most of our humanness is lost.

For many, the deeper process, the 'unconscious' does not exist. I cannot count the times someone has told me they do not dream. When I say that is impossible, they should be mad or dead, they then say they can't remember them or they are meaningless nonsense. Little wonder, in the face of this neglect that their deeper process remains hidden. To live without knowledge of the deeper process is to float, anchorless, on an ocean of experience without ever looking down.

Most therapy aims to help different parts of a person connect and communicate. I will stop a client in mid story and ask them to notice what is going on inside. As they find an unnoticed inner meaning to their narrative, their experience becomes fuller and richer. Sometimes I will sense that a client has brought a dream and has forgotten to tell me. I try to help them recognize the riches they are ignoring—create a space for the deeper process to be heard.

We may not be able to hold the different levels in our awareness at the same time but we can learn to sample the quality of each, regularly and naturally. To be stuck in any process is unhealthy, even if it is an aspect of the Greater process.

I worked with an adolescent boy who got lost in a 'spiritual crisis.' There was no doubt he was in touch with a reality from which profound wisdom flowed. He knew astounding things about the inner nature of those around him; he could speak with authority about life. But he was trapped, and his immature body and mind could not contain the outpouring of energy. Diagnosed as hypomanic he was prescribed drugs to bring him down to our shared reality. Sad as he was to lose that visionary experience, the decision to ground him was what he needed for his ordinary life.

All levels of our being have to become more related. That is the path toward integration and wholeness. So as you read and think about these processes, aim to put it all together, not only in your mind but also in your experience. Remember incidents and events that are characteristic, which evoke the essence of each level for you. Let it become real.

The Greater Process

Religious and mystical literature offers a tantalizing but elusive vision of reality. In that divine universe there is no separation, no self and no suffering. Everything is one, indivisible, complete, and unified. Many of us struggle with that vision, yearning for some ultimate truth, yet embarrassed by the irrationality of religious dogma. There seems little space for transcendence amidst the daily demands of life. And to whom would we talk about those precious yearnings, that "still small voice" we hear inside?

People nowadays speak more easily about their intimate sexual exploits than their spiritual experiences and aspirations. The enigmatic, the inexplicable, the inexpressible are powerfully repressed. The pressure to conform, to be 'normal' is intense.

After many months of therapy I got a hint that an ex-Catholic woman, as a youth, shared my yearnings to become a saint. She would pour over "The Lives of the Saints," pray fervently, do penance and 'good works.' By the age of eighteen that powerful yearning was tattered and discarded—her naïve sense of the transcendent had gone underground. As she confessed to that devotion in the session, her face glowed red with embarrassment. Much as she wished to deny it, that thirst for the divine was still with her, but obscured.

The Greater process is inaccessible because we fail to notice the extraordinary in the ordinary. Everyone tastes sacredness at some time. But do we value those 'big' dreams, odd coincidences, subtle intuitions, and intense connections that sprinkled our lives? Are we willing to notice the mystery all around us?

The most common brush with the Greater process comes during immersion in nature. The immediacy of water, earth, air, vegetation and animal invite us to connect. For some this is too overwhelming and unsettling; they talk louder, walk faster, cycle harder to maintain their sense of small self in the face of all that vastness. To know the Greater process we have to settle, get quiet inside, put away the distractions and allow ourselves to expand. Then a Presence makes itself known.

This Presence comes unexpectedly. We can only invite, not control. A birth or death, great joy or sorrow, creates a doorway, an opening, for that contact to be made. Jillian, working through the most terrifying abuse, was touched one night by a "being of light." She was filled with a healing peace. Jim recalled his old experiences of hearing celestial music. That memory became a soothing companion through periods of despair and emptiness.

Dreams and Synchronicity

Dreams are a wonderful doorway to another world. I have been witness to a multitude of life changing dreams that point toward the transcendent. Certain ones stay in mind. Julia was riddled with cancer when she dreamed of a glorious golden tree sweeping over a rainbow pool, drawing up light that ever-flowed through the branches and leaves to return to that pool; she died not long after. In a time of darkness Mark was visited by a giant "Wise One" who surrounded him with protective wings; slowly he began to accept the reality of his deep spirituality. For Rhona, a pool of solid darkness, that is both the beginning and end of a river, invites her to baptism and renewal. She must take care not to stay immersed too long or she may never return to shore.

The unusual, the strange and the coincidental that summon us to awareness visits all. In C. G. Jung's terms these are synchronistic happenings—inner and outer experiences connected, not by ordinary causes, but by some other joining force. One client, again in a dream, was given a detailed picture of the inside of a house that she visited for the first time the following week. She was only surprised when she found that the telephone was slightly out of place than she remembered. We think of someone just as they call us, know that something is happening to a loved one many miles away. There is no scientific explanation for these common experiences but that does not make them less true.

More often we are visited by the Greater process disguised in the shape of the ordinary. An illness, a car accident, an unexpected meeting are prompts and hints that something more is going on. Not long ago I literally bumped into an old girl friend at an airport carousel. We had been out of touch for eighteen years; something unfinished was left between us. I turned around and she was there, suddenly transported across the miles and years. What was that meeting for? Why was this happening to me at just this moment? What was its meaning? Those are the question we should ask about every event that grabs our attention.

Without some point of contact with the Greater process, whatever we name it, life becomes ultimately meaningless. Whether we espouse it in scientific laws, natural beauty, human relationship, religion or social activism, does not matter. What is important is a sense of something greater, more encompassing, less selfish and narrow—something of which we are a part. A pattern of belonging exists in the universe and it keeps trying to remind us.

We know the transcendent better as we become more whole —it slips away as we are lost in the byways of living. With increasing awareness, we begin to connect all parts of ourselves in a gentle harmony with the *way things are*, with the flow of life. Then we take on meaning like ballast. No longer tossed around by the winds of fate, the water of life calms. Decisions grow simpler: "Is it right for me, my family and the whole; is this the direction of my life path, or is it a diversion?" Attunement with the Greater process brings peace and tranquility; life becomes richer and fuller.

The Deeper Process

The Greater process connects most closely with that which is deep within. That is why we so often receive guidance through dreams. Emerging out of the whole, the deeper process serves as the foundation for our individual being. Yet it is impersonal and often implacable in the demands it makes on us.

I imagine the deeper process as a tree, naturally ruthless, rooting deep into the earth splitting rocks, growing upward and outward regardless of hindrance. The deeper process is not careful of our feelings or our outer life; it just goes about its business of keeping us alive and growing. If our personality gets in the way, it will be pushed aside. If we do not learn readily then maybe a stronger wake-up call is needed.

Those who ignored more subtle warnings are often visited by overwhelming and unavoidable life crises. The deeper process first whispers in our ear, then taps us on the shoulder. Finally, if we still won't listen, it gets out the baseball bat! I have seen a number of men who after years of empty relationship were shocked and overwhelmed when their partners left. Their self-deception was finally shattered by undeniable reality. Now they had to change.

Heart attacks, autoimmune disease, chronic undiagnosed fatigue, even massive allergic reactions can be a wake-up call from another part of our being. A narrow and controlling man came to see me because of sexual problems. All he wanted was for me to help him get back his ability to have an erection. He had recently been diagnosed with scleroderma, a tragic disease that causes the whole of the skin to lose elasticity; his psychological rigidity was manifesting all over his body. Our work together helped relax the demands he made on himself and others and softened his approach to life. He began to accept that there were forces in his being that cannot be controlled.

The deeper process keeps us alive, preserving our physical and psychological well-being. But rather than simply maintaining the status quo, it pushes in the direction of growth and integration. If our life is blocked, so is our vitality. If we do not make the next step forward in life, we may end up literally unable to move.

We cannot escape the influence of the deeper process; it is ever-present and watching. Research shows that an unconscious part of us is constantly vigilant. When we are about to step off the sidewalk in front of a speeding truck, it pulls us back. Almost half a second before we are aware, some other part responds to important information from the environment.[2] The conscious mind may think it is in control but it often functions to ratify decisions already made beneath awareness. Often, what we believe is informed choice is, in effect, agreement, or disagreement with the deeper process. We forget that the deeper process emerged first as the carrier wave of our identity, long before the self came on the scene. It naturally takes precedence.

Dysfunction and Misunderstandings

In infancy, the deeper process is eager to get the different human systems up and running—moving, talking, relating, and learning. We are like vacuum cleaners, we take everything in—into our mouths and into our souls. Much of what we ingest is nourishing; it becomes part of us. But some energies and experiences are overwhelming and toxic.

Everything sinks downward. The unconscious becomes the repository of all that has fallen out of awareness—the good, the bad and the ugly. It does its best to make sense of it all, but oftentimes fails. Then certain elements have to be partitioned off, hidden away or awkwardly cobbled together.

This gives rise to strange misconceptions, like the one at the root of Bob's depression. We knew it had something to do with his father's death when Bob was four years old, but he did not consciously remember any details. In a hypnotic regression it began to make sense.

Bobby had been naughty and his father had gotten annoyed. Later that day there was a commotion downstairs. An ambulance arrived and Bobby was told to stay in his room. He came out, saw his aunt sobbing and knew something terrible had happened. His father never came back and Bobby was told Dad had died of a heart attack. It was obvious to little Bobby that he had caused it— his naughtiness had *attacked his daddy's heart*. Daddy had died and gone away forever because of him.

This childish misunderstanding caused a severe blockage in Bob's life energy. Some part of him believed that to be vigorous, energetic and alive was to be naughty—and naughty was very dangerous as it might kill those he loved. Reconnecting this hidden experience to Bob's adult self created a new way for him to experience. He could be more himself.

Whatever the task, the deeper process never gives up its attempts to make us whole. Whatever lies undigested will be regurgitated whenever there is the slightest chance for change. That is why we become emotionally 'triggered' by certain situations. Semi-autonomous patterns take over our thinking, feeling, and actions. Automatic, primitive urges—far different from our conscious wishes—catch and bind us. Our reaction to particular situations gets way out of proportion.

Such are the compulsive responses that catch us off guard. Someone cuts me off in traffic and I respond immediately with a burst of anger. If I completely let go, I might give in to "road rage" and do something stupid. Looking at it later, I tell myself I lost it. I try to think of some convenient rationalization that makes me look a bit better—I was stressed, the other guy was a jerk, and it was the last straw. The whole thing quickly fades from memory.

What actually happened is that I was *gripped*. For a short time something had taken over and I was not myself. That 'something' is a disconnected aspect of the deeper process intruding into my inner and outer life. In Jungian terminology this is called a *complex*—a semi-autonomous aspect of our psyche that takes over when triggered.

Why this happens is complicated. At one level it simply reflects my obvious dissociation and disturbances; it shows I am not whole. At another level, it is an attempt to have something change. The compulsive reaction recreates, on the outside, a situation that parallels an unresolved issue that exists deeper within. It is an opportunity, a crisis that hopes for a different and resolving outcome.

As that person raging in his car, I may be re-experiencing some of the powerlessness I felt in the face of an intrusive parent. I may be forced to confront my overbearing childish sense of entitlement. I may be replaying anger at the world that never gave me what I needed. If I catch this hint from within, something may reconnect; its intent has been realized. If I ignore the invitation to awareness, it will surely re-present itself at the earliest opportunity.

Our cyclical, disturbing patterns are no different from recurring dreams. Whenever a dream or nightmare perturbs us, we are actually being invited to notice and do something. Ignoring that invitation, the dream will recur. Once a repetitive dream is worked with sufficiently, once the message is received and acted on, the dream will never present itself in the same form; the pattern has changed.

As a young child I was tormented by a nightmare that came again and again. In it, the lines on my pillow stretched out into the infinite darks of space, never touching, never connecting. I now recognize that dream as an early attempt to understand why my parents could never make real contact with each other. In the dream I was desperate for those parallel lines to simply touch, to come together finally—but they never did. Over the years, as I accepted the reality of how my parents were, the dream faded.

Night dreams mostly do their work without conscious help. The twilight descent into realms of unconsciousness puts us back together; without it we get sick or crazy. All the stages of sleep, from dreaming REM to the deepest recuperative sleep cycles, are absolutely essential.[3] The inner and outer processes become quiescent during this time allowing for maintenance and repair.

The deeper process is always awake; we are always dreaming. Many times during a day we graze the edge of the unconscious—pondering, daydreaming, musing, and drifting.[4] Mostly we shake ourselves awake and erase those images from memory. We forget to recall that we have journeyed elsewhere.

When the deeper process is present in awareness, it swirls and flows with strange thoughts, snatches of songs and half-remembered stories. Images arise from the back of our minds—magical, primitive, evocative, even scary. If these turn against us, we are without recourse. We cannot shift an irrational fear through wishing; obsession grips us against our will. The deeper process has the power to make us sick or well, fearful or confident. When it is our friend, when we know it intimately, anything is possible.

The Inner Process

Waking each day, we emerge out of deep sleep into an in-between place of shifting thoughts and dream-like images. We are crossing the border between the deeper and the inner process. One begins and the other ends at a fuzzy boundary where experience exists in a kind of twilight awareness.[5]

Take a moment some morning as you wake. Without moving, review what is swimming past your inner eye. You may notice that it is a strange mixture of dream and thought. If you begin to think about some outer concern—say, what you have to do later—then your awareness is drawn toward waking. If you begin to slide back into your dreams, before you know it you have drifted off for a few minutes.

Staying in that state, you can recapture unremembered information, be taken by an unusual idea or suffer from an anxious preoccupation. It is a place of choice and choicelessness, of the real and the phantasmagoric, the benign and the frightful. Evoked in therapy through imagery or light hypnosis, it is used to find what is lost, hidden, or inarticulate. Like casting a net into the sea, strange beings of many shapes get drawn to the surface of our inner process.

The inner process creates the sense of who we are; all those ideas, expectations, subjective feelings and intuitions that are close to the bone of our identity. These are our self-concepts, our feelings of self-worth and bodily experiences that fuse together into that insistent yet amorphous inner experience of personal identity—the *self*.[6] The self is not a thing or even a being. It is a wave-like work in progress, a compromise between what is, what has been, and what may arise.

When a client enters the office I sometimes ask, "How are you?" This is both a trivial and non-trivial question. The answer tells me not only how they are feeling but who they are at that moment. If I get the superficial reply, "Fine", I may ask the same question again but with different emphasis: "How *are* you?" I usually get a more penetrating response. If I want to keep pushing inward, I ask the more difficult question, "How are *you*?" The person will hesitate momentarily. I notice a switch of awareness, an inward search. The answer will be unforeseen. It will reflect processes closer to the sense of self.

All experience is measured against existing core aspects of 'selfness.' Each is assigned a 'feeling tone'—a judgment of value, relevance and connection. You tell yourself, without words, whether what you experience is more or less 'like you.'[7] As happenings intrude from the world—or from deeper—some will be ignored or rejected while others are welcomed and connected to what already exists within.

Think of something you did or said that was humiliating. Maybe you can still feel the hot flush of embarrassment. That bodily reaction tells you that your action still does not fit comfortably with who you think you are. You would rather it never happened; it activates your defenses.

We are all defensive; we absolutely need a protective boundary around our fragile self. Like a middleman, the inner process lies between the deeper and outer. Influenced on all sides, it seeks to create an equilibrium of opposite and impinging forces. Its task is to sustain a sense of identity that works in the world, yet is open to the riches and appetites that bubble up from beneath.

No wonder our self experiences confusion, conflict and doubt. At any moment, we may be trapped between the 'shoulds' of outer responsibility and the 'wants' of our deeper needs—between deferred gratification and insistent entitlement. The self is a precarious balance of compromise and coordination.

The Self in Relationship

Think of the important experiences that have contributed to your sense of who you are. They almost certainly are experiences of relationship. Who were the influential people and groups in your life—family, teachers, mentors, friends?

When our self is developing, we seek guidance and companionship, and some way to define who we are. *Belonging* helps; it bolsters an inner process that is immature and sensitive. Connecting with others, we begin to find out who we might be. Adolescents need peer groups to try on different personalities. Adults gain identity from work groups, church membership, community or political affiliation. We all need to belong; we all need to define ourselves. But we also must grow beyond belonging, beyond definition.

76

We grow through relationship, particularly relationship with ourselves. It takes time and courage to face and know who we are. For many, solitude and aloneness are mixed up with loneliness— an intolerable sense of being incomplete. So we seek completeness through others; we are compelled into relationship. Yet it is only when we can tolerate, accept and appreciate ourselves alone that we enter into healthy connection with others.

True relationship requires that we come to it as whole as possible. When two or more relatively intact people join, something extraordinary happens. There is a synergy, a vitality that takes the participants beyond themselves into the transpersonal. This is the sacred meaning of marriage and true friendship.

Because we are not yet whole, because parts of our being are not in agreement and fragmented, we have difficulty being whole-hearted in relationship. Mostly we look for a connection, a relationship that can soothe the hurts that have not healed. Seeking to feel more complete, we use the other person to fill in the gaps, the empty places inside. Unless we face our inner demons, do our inner work, our brokenness will be reflected back by whomever we are with.

Many try to side-step the demands of inner work by focussing on outer achievement and success. No matter how effective we are in the world, regardless of how creative or artistic, if our inner process is not resilient and whole, we will still feel lost. Do you pay enough attention to what is happening inside? Do you allow yourself to be distracted by external concerns that have little real substance?

I mentioned a wealthy client, Jason, previously. In therapy he could never sit still. He would pace around the room, peer at objects on my shelves, comment on my decor. At some point in our conversation he would inevitably introduce some oblique comment that reminded me of how many things he owned. He was so terrified of stopping and looking at his life, that he had to keep on the move like a restless animal. Distorted, far out of harmony, his inner experience was torture. Nothing on the outside could protect him from his suffering.

With maturity, for most of us, our sense of self becomes more substantial. We are less often tormented by doubts and fears. As experiences come together there is a smoother flow, a clearer stream. The inner process does its job with less complaint. We move outward, explore the possibilities and complexities of our world. The outer process has inner support, the foundation it requires.

The Outer Process

The inner and outer are designed to work in tandem. Without an inner self, without a sense of valuing and feeling, the world is a barren wasteland of empty activity. Then again, without the stimulation of the world, the abrasion and incarnation of the physical, our inner feelings become a stagnant pool. We become emotionally constipated. An emotion is incomplete if not expressed. Thought demands action. The outer life is a container for our desires and creative impulses. We need it to live and grow.

The *substance* of our lives is lived in the material world. We are born into a body, subject to physical forces and needs. That body has to be nourished and cared for—without it we cease to exist. Life demands that we be active, move, work and make things happen. There is no alternative. How we accomplish all this, the style and manner of our being in the world is the work of our outer process.

Each of us is a composite of the specific and the universal, the unique and the commonplace, the individual and the general. Born into a human form, like other human forms, we are designed to see, hear, feel, move, and talk, in a similar way to all other humans. Our family and culture shape us to conform to what is 'normal.' We are enjoined to pay attention to certain 'essential' things, to dress appropriately, to be productive and efficient, to see the world as others do. Yet each person is different from every other being that ever existed. I am unique, you are unique, and we can never have exactly the same experiences.

We enter this collective world with our own style of being, our own characteristic nature. Some personalities are tough, extroverted, outgoing. Others are sensitive, introverted, and retiring.[8] The same event and the perception of that event will never have exactly the same meaning to two different people. So each new life brings with it both innovation and the potential for conflict and misunderstanding. A domineering executive may become disgusted with her sensitive daughter who prefers homemaking and dolls to intellectual pursuits. Quiet, sedate parents may have no idea how to cope with a lively, vital five-year-old boy—especially if he is so unlike the 'well-behaved' child that came first. He is likely to be a problem, be labeled as hyperactive and medicated.

Too often parental expectations and a child's way of being disagree—a clash between how the child is and how she is supposed to be. Her relationship with the world is endangered and issues of success and failure grow large and insurmountable. The child has a hard time finding her own sense of direction, her own pace of working, or a way of life that fits.

Dawn could never adjust to the parental mold. She was too big, too un-ladylike and too ebullient. From the earliest age she loved to draw on every surface with any crayon, marker or pencil that came to hand. She remembers at the age of three being sent to her room for marking a wall—all drawing materials forbidden. At seven she brought home some precious paintings from school. Her mother said, "How nice", but the next day Dawn found them crumpled in the garbage.

Her parents were not mean or nasty—they just had no idea who she was, or why certain things were important to her. She came home from summer camp at age thirteen to find her room redecorated with flowery wallpaper and ruffles on the bed. Her soft toy companions had disappeared. She hated it all. But what was she to say when her mother was so enthusiastic and smug?

When I saw her as an adult in her thirties, Dawn's creativity was blocked. She had escaped the claustrophobic home to go to art school. There every painting became a torture of self-doubt. Now married, with a growing child, she had time to pursue her artistic dreams. Constantly self-critical, she could not complete even one product. The cycle of creativity—inspiration, expression, action, accomplishment—remained unfulfilled. No matter what the inner desire and urgency, her outer process would not respond. Dawn was unable to find the connection between her inner vision and her outer competence. She kept getting in her own way.

Did you fit in your family? Did they recognize and appreciate the unique contribution that you brought to the world? It is the subtle and often unspoken attitudes of adults that influence how a child will be in their outer life. Doors are closed, never to reopen. The gulf between inner nature and outer achievement becomes an impassible dangerous chasm.

As outer concerns take over more and more of the person, as unawareness grows, evil can gain a foothold. I am reminded of a mother who ignored her intuition, ignored the evidence of her husband's obsessive interest in their daughter. Many years later she learned of the sexual abuse. Her regrets still haunt her.

That mother was busy, constantly cleaning and tidying. Her outer process had colonized the whole of her life and attention. If *doing* is given too great a domination, it takes over—anything other than endless striving hardly registers. Is this your life?

Money

The demands and reality of the world appear undeniable. Yet apart from physical requirements, most of our outer experience is culturally determined. Those things we take for granted—work, leisure, automobiles, cuisine, marriage, and families—are 'made up' by our society. From the moment of birth we are socialized into accepting the status quo, the unquestionable collective reality. Group ideas about how things should be get a stranglehold on our being. Preeminent among all the cultural creations that control us in the West is *money*.

I often have to discuss finances with clients. It is usually a difficult conversation. As a client squirms in his seat, I know he would prefer to talk about anything else—sex and death are welcome, lighter topics. I asked one woman why she always put the check for the session face down on my desk. She replied, "I will never sort out my money issues in this lifetime." Another man who was having financial troubles burst into tears when I suggested he might ask for a sliding scale for session fees.

Money is worldly power and money is worldly choice. The amount we own determines many aspects of our life—whether we eat, have a car and home, go on vacation, see a therapist. Most of us spend half our waking lives in pursuit of financial rewards. We exchange our time, our energy, and our expertise for dollars. So what is it that we are giving half our lives for?

Certainly money is not a thing. It is not those green pieces of paper, not writing on a check, not numbers on a bank statement and not gold in Fort Knox. All of those things become meaningless in a moment if we have lost faith and trust in them. The great financial crash in Germany between the wars shows the truth. Money is an unconscious agreement, an expectation of value that can be transferred between people. It exists more in our group mind than in the material universe. It is made up, but like a child's fearful fantasy, it has an oppressive force.

Money is a good metaphor for our outer process. Winifred Rushforth, at the age of ninety-seven wrote a book called *Life's Currency: Time Money and Energy*.[9] In it , she says that how we relate to any one of these aspects in our lives reflects our relationship with all of them. Our approach to money gives us insight into how we 'spend' our time and our life energy. The pattern of our outer process is laid bare.

We need to constantly ask ourselves: How do I use my time, my energy, my money? What is my relationship with the world—the stuff, the people, the events, the activities that make up my outer life?" Is the pursuit of financial reward taking up too much of my time and experience?

Our abilities obviously influence how well we do in life. But that is not the whole story; our attitudes and expectations are equally important. Riches do not come to us by wishing for them—we have to work. But without the necessary energetic intention, much of what we do will be ineffectual. We can drive away money and success by subtly neglecting opportunities, by disdaining "filthy lucre" and by never believing that we deserve positive fortune. I know this from my family experience.

My grandfather and his fathers before him were landowners in Wales. Never having to work for what he owned, he wasted a fortune through neglect. My own father inherited a tendency to financial negligence. He forgets to pay bills and avoids asking for what he is owed. After a long struggle with this legacy, I have learned to stay within the reality of my finances. It requires a certain quality of attention—not anxious, not obsessive, not avoidant but lively interest and appreciation. It is not so different from gardening: the beds must be dug, the seeds planted in the right season, the tender seedlings nurtured, and the harvest enjoyed.

I see a similar struggle in some clients. One who has tremendous ambivalence about her free-lance work often has droves of customers cancel on her. This always happens whenever she wants to avoid working. The customers give ordinary excuses, they are sick or unable to come, but somehow the universe is responding to her negativity. When she is able to harness her feelings the clients call again.

Facing Outer Reality

I am not suggesting that our attitudes simply control outer events. At times in our lives we are faced by overwhelming situations. Therapists see more than their fair share of the harsh side of living, the shadow of humanity. Ordinary people are suddenly blind-sided, smashed into by unforeseen events: a young child dies, a mother develops cancer, the family home is burned to the ground.

These things happen—and happen often and unexpectedly. No one is immune. It is no use pretending that you and I are special or protected, that disaster only strikes others. We are often too scared to look life's dark side fully in the face, so we use partial denial, subtle avoidance to make it more palatable. This is the normal 'manic defense' that allows each of us to carry on without succumbing to terror or depression. How could we drive a car on a highway if we kept remembering the high probability of being killed? Somehow we have to live with the awareness that bad things may happen to us.

Avoidance of inevitable truths, frantic and vain attempts to achieve security cause the outer process to go awry. We have to confront a stark fact: *we are not in control.* Events happen, the world changes, disaster strikes, and we all die sometime. Life *will* kill us sooner or later. If we cannot control and we cannot avoid, then how should we respond to life?

If we live on the surface, in only the outer shell of life, then there is no answer. As we connect with all dimensions of our being we begin to see a glimmer of light. That light is the luminous flow of connected wholeness. This is not the fragile flicker of belief or faith, serving as a bastion against life's perils; it is a matter of experience. Only experience is certain—not just experience of parts of ourselves, but that of everything altogether.

Peter had dedicated his life to spiritual practice. He had

traveled to India, meditated in remote places and lived in an ashram for many years. Now in his late forties, his spiritual teacher had told him it was time to find his feet in the world. For all his spiritual journeying, he was still incomplete; he had not entered fully into the work of this world. He returned to the United States to learn computing and face the stress of starting his own business, to fulfill a neglected aspect of life. Now he could bring his calm insight into every contact with customers and into every minute of each day.

Life is a moment to moment affair. Embedded within each moment is the possibility of manifesting life's essence, its wholeness, the Greater process. When all our processes reconnect back to the Greater process, the circle is complete—experience becomes imbued with meaning and light. Drudgery and boredom, fear and strife are symptoms of our disconnection. Vitality and enjoyment are our true inheritance.

Living in Process

Being human is not simple. Exploring our humanness cannot be simplistic. We are creatures of many dimensions, distinct, yet part of a greater whole. We live simultaneously in many different worlds. We have to pay attention to the requirements of each of these worlds—and the way they connect together.

The outer world is the 'landscape' of our life, a world of material reality that constantly impinges on us. The texture of our outer experience, our outer process, influences how we respond to what happens to us and what we do about it. We have to act. Through action a difference is created whose ripples extend out into the future. Every deed changes the universe.

Being in the world is a sacred responsibility, a duty to become increasingly aware of the consequences of everything we do. It is not enough to think of our own interests or those of our family and community. We have to realize the interconnectedness of the universe, act as if each moment is of ultimate importance. That only becomes possible if we remember that we are human beings.[10]

This remembering is the *inscape* of experiencing, the 'innerness' of who we feel we are. Feelings, values, choices, decisions are the essence of this inner realm of subjectivity. "Know Thyself" was written over the doorway of the Delphic oracle; there is no better advice. So how are we to follow that advice? Become aware of what is happening within—not just occasionally but often, every moment we have a chance.

Knowing who we are means not succumbing to self-deception, not giving in to egotism and inflation or even its opposite— feelings of inadequacy and false humility. Balance is everything; a realistic and honest view of who we are and what we are capable of is an essential gift. Whenever we entertain a distorted view of ourselves, either too much or too little, we lose our center. The negative voice that criticizes ourselves or others acts out of fear and defensiveness. It closes us to love and connection.

The inner world needs connection, needs the richness of relationship. It keeps us supple, it is essential exercise for the heart. So every time we reach out and feel that connection, whether it is with a person, a work of art or nature, something is added to our inner experiencing. Not just love or attraction but also dislike, disgust, even hate are all good exercise if we stay aware. We should never hide from the experiences that seek us out. Every feeling or urge has something to tell us about who we are.

The inner and outer processes are personal to each of us. They create our individual experience and make up the texture of our distinctive way of being and doing. The deeper process belongs to the unconscious dimensions, the fluid and formless *underworld*, the stuff of myth and nature.

This is a natural and impersonal world. In the same way that every living being grows into a particular form, so nature shapes us beyond our will or awareness. When experience arises out of this realm it feels *other*; it does not belong to who we think we are. Our dreams are filled with narratives that seem foreign to our waking concerns. Images and urges, creativity and invention surge into consciousness, beyond control or intention.

How are we to relate to that impersonal aspect of our being? In the previous chapter I suggested that the deeper process responds to trust and respect; it requires that we make the effort to listen deeply. Rather than discarding or discounting the subtle prompting, we should welcome them with awe and curiosity. We have to pierce the veil of obscurity that shrouds our dreams—write them, paint them, look around in the world for objects and experiences that match the images.

There is a technique in hypnosis called by the formidable name, "idiomotor signaling."[11] In essence, while a person is in a hypnotic trance, the therapist can ask the unconscious, deeper self of the client to signal "Yes", "No", "Maybe", by small, movements of different parts of the body, most often the fingers. The client is seldom fully aware of these movements which are clearly observable. So I might help a client in a trance to explore deeper blocks to physical healing by asking simple yes/no questions: "Is there some hidden reasons that X cannot get well? Are these reasons physical? Are they emotional? Do these reasons come from experiences earlier in life?" In this way I begin to ferret out the agenda of the deeper process.

This technique clearly shows how our unconscious has access to all sorts of information and memories that are normally unavailable to consciousness. "We know much more than we think we know," as Milton Erickson, the master hypnotherapist, would say. In actuality, the deeper process is signaling all the time through subtle movements, changes in the way we feel and responses to the energies and atmospheres surrounding us. You might say that the unconscious keeps up a silent running commentary about everything that goes on.

Tuning in to this communication requires that we sense our

body and notice minute shifts and changes as they occur. With practice, most can discover their own way to access an inner knowing. Then we realize the wisdom, power, and knowledge of our deeper process. It is waiting for us to get in touch.

That can also be said about the Greater process. But rather than a natural impersonal aspect of our being, the Greater process is transpersonal—beyond and greater than individual experience. The quality is different, more refined, encompassing and complete. While we sense the deeper process as organic, visceral, downward, and obscure, the greater process is experienced as up and out, light, bright, impalpable and enlivening. Unexpectedly interceding in our everyday experience, a new life within our life, it takes us out of our limited selves into something greater.

The more a person attunes with the Greater process, the more that person seems 'together.' I think of that state as *single minded, whole-hearted and utterly embodied.* A person who is 'all of a piece' carries a personal presence of coherence, serenity and flow. Whatever we do to increase that alignment of body, heart, mind, and action increases our ability to be present. The flowering of presence is the unitive experience.

For a few saintly souls, this state may be relatively permanent. For most of us it is at best transitory. We catch a glimpse of how we could be before returning to our normally dissonant mode. Living in tune with the Greater process is the goal of religion, of spiritual disciplines, and of the right path in life. It is the Way of Taoism, the Dharma of Buddhists, surrender to Allah in Islam, the path of beauty for the Navajo Indians, the grace of the Holy Spirit, the influx of the Life Force. With many names and many faces, it all leads in the same direction—toward wholeness.

Scattered throughout the spiritual literature of the world are hints and clues on how to connect with a Greater reality. Certainly we cannot command the transcendent; it is far beyond our wishes, desires and spiritual tricks. To believe we can entrap enlightenment through any particular practice is like a leaf trying to capture the wind. The Greater process manifests when we are ready and when we have created enough space to experience beyond what we think is possible. Then we can surrender.

We do this by growing more fully into ourselves. We invite the Greater process into our lives by becoming the most we can, by connecting all the dimensions of our being. As we become more *of* who we are, we become more *than* we are.

PART II

How We Become
Who We Are

CHAPTER 5

The Thread of Life

Man should not ask what he may expect from life, but should rather understand that life expects something from him.
—Victor Frankl

What you have to attempt—to be yourself. What you have to pray for—to become a mirror in which, according to the degree of purity of heart you have attained, the greatness of life will be reflected.
—Dag Hammarskjöld

Can you recall your first memory? Mine is from age two. I am toddling into my mother's room. I look up onto the bed where my mother, clad in a blue nightgown, is breast-feeding a tiny baby, my newborn brother. I have an overwhelming, indescribable feeling that travels like a wave through my body.

From my current viewpoint that feeling is both mine and not mine. That toddler is me and not me. Who I am now is connected to that experience in a subtle yet irrefutable way. There is a thread of continuity that connects that child and this adult, binding us into one continuous being.

Our sense of self is very obvious, very current. We seem to know who we are and remain convinced that we will stay that way for the foreseeable future. A strange illusion hides our changing reality behind a mask of stability. As living beings we are moving, flowing patterns of energy. Our bodies have no individual cell older than a few years, our minds are labyrinths of ceaselessly skipping thoughts, our feelings change like sunshine behind clouds. Yet an essential unity links the fetus in the womb with a little child growing up, the adult you are now and the older person you will become.

There is an image that comes from the teachings of Ouspensky, a disciple of the charismatic Gurdjieff.[1] It captures our outstretched identity expressed in a whole life, from conception to demise. For Ouspensky, the extended self is four dimensional, a *long body*. It exists simultaneously across time and space as a tube-like form, twisting and turning through all the moments of our life and through all the places we live and visit.

Imagine yourself elongated in time, like the comic character "Flash" who moves so fast his multiple images trail behind him. Wherever you were and will be is a body-shaped cross section of your *long body*. Like a flowing sinuous afterimage, you are still in your bed last night, still eating breakfast tomorrow. You are there at your birthing, there on your deathbed—at all the places and all the times of your life. Who you are is every experience of every instant.

In a therapy session, I sample the momentary flow of a client's process. But that sample is a tiny portion of the whole person. Long-term psychotherapy, over many years, furnishes a growing sense of the shape of a life. Hour by therapeutic hour, we link together a person's experiences. Conception, birth, and early childhood are the foundation. Then each succeeding period with its particular dilemmas, its specific developmental needs and tasks. The struggles and successes, the opportunities—missed or grasped—the life-long learnings, are all part of it. Every joy, each moment of despair—loves, hopes, fears—are woven into the unique pattern that is this person, here with me now. That pattern has its own inimitable shape.

Many clients feel an intense need to recollect their life, to piece together the forgotten, lost and mislaid. Jillian wrote a superb book chronicling her history. She had taken years to recover the worst of her childhood abuse and make sense of it. Some of the chapters were gut wrenching—others awe inspiring. Knowing her so well, I was still surprised by the weight of detail, the intricate recurring patterns.

Another woman circled the walls of her dining room with a thirty-foot long sheet of butcher's paper. On it she drew her 'life-line', divided into months and years. Above the line she put in the main events of her life, below she wrote how she had felt and reacted. The patterns and obscure connections became increasingly apparent. She learned more about herself in that six-month project than in years of therapy.

How would you express the flowing form of your life? Can you feel the thread of continuity that connects your infancy with the present and with your old age? Do you know your 'long body'? Many of us lose that thread, feel distant from our earliest self. At best we can remember the scattered islands of events that define our life. Most experiences prior to the age of four are shrouded. Yet nothing is totally gone, all is potentially redeemable—but like a chaotic filing system, we are at a loss how to retrieve the information.

Painful life events cause a fraying or tear in the fabric of our identity. We do not want to feel that pain again so we do not look in that direction. If our life remains unexamined and incomplete, however, we cannot make sense of who we are and the way we experience.[2] Our dysfunctions remain meaningless and intractable; our unrealized potentials stagnate, locked in some unexplored cave of our being.

The Long Body

Bonsai trees fascinate me; I have a miniature juniper under the window in my office. Regardless of the restrictions, it keeps trying to grow toward the form of its essential nature—to become the most tree possible. Each 'abuse'—clipping, training, manipulation of light and fertilizer—is integrated as best it can by the little tree into a new attempt to develop fully. The result is contorted yet profoundly beautiful.

Like the Bonsai, we are a compromise between our inherent nature and the demands of the world. All influences, from the most subtle to the most gross, are incorporated into our being. From the moment of conception, physical and energetic forces impinge on our being. Some of these help us grow while others misshape us.

Alive in the womb, we are enveloped by the unthinking experiences of our mother. What she ingests becomes our body. The love and conflict between our parents is the hormonal fluid in which we bathe. For the fetus, 40 weeks of gestation is a whole lifetime beset with a multitude of events, some soothing and nurturing and others harsh and unforgiving. Then to cap it all, we are expelled naked from the safety of the womb.

When we explore the deeper process in therapy, there is a place in each of us that knows whether we were welcome in this world.[3] Clients come to grasp somatically, 'in their gut', whether their parents were terrified, ambivalent or overjoyed by the pregnancy. Some feel they never should have been born; it is too hard to be embodied. They have been delivered without any 'psychological skin'—a rawness to the inevitable friction and discomfort of living. Being in a body, in this world, is a constant irritation and anguish. Little wonder they do not feel at home.

We all carry within ourselves a deep knowing that there is an *elsewhere* that is simple, nurturing and so unlike here. Sometimes all we want is to go back.

This *life phobia* reflects a profound spiritual issue. As one extremely sensitive woman put it, "I did not sign up for this world when I agreed to be born. It is just too hard." We can imagine her in the spirit world excited by the prospect of taking a new life, only to be deeply disappointed and shocked by its harshness and difficulty. No wonder she wants to get out of here, to return to a simpler experience, whether womb or waiting room of the soul. But there is no going back. The embodied spirit has been forcefully ejected. Such is being born.

Birth

Birth is not inherently traumatizing. Birth is a natural process, an entry portal into the world. For the infant, being born is the most extraordinary and life-changing event that has ever occurred. Physically demanding for both participants, the baby is prepared to be fully engaged and involved in that transition between worlds. The massive adrenaline rush during labor kick-starts the infant into a new awareness, into a different way of experiencing. When it all works, the infant arrives wide-eyed and open to whatever life may bring.

Orianne's labor started early on an overcast June morning. We relaxed in bed while the hot-tub heated and then spent a peaceful and sanctified time together in the warm waters, practicing all the skills we had learned. Time slipped by so smoothly and quietly we almost forgot to call the midwives before it was too late. By the time they arrived, second stage was upon us; we moved inside to the birthing room. Two hours of intensely hard work and our daughter, Marisha was born. Emanuel, our seven year old son, was ushered in to cut the cord and we were now a family of four—a true blessing and confirmation of all the prayer and preparation we had invested.

Birthing is a sacred time. It requires the most careful attention to the subtleties of atmosphere, attitude and action. Sacraments are defined in Christian Catholicism as "outward signs of inward grace." Inner as well as outer preparation is needed for all sacred events. The effort and work involved for mother and child (and father) is a shared ordeal bonding them together. There is great risk and potential for incredible joy. The miracle of a new life is happening and it demands the utmost reverence.

Reverence may be the ideal but it is not always the reality. Too often childbirth has been treated as a medical problem, an emergency requiring cold instruments, drugs and surgery. The mother feels unprotected and unprepared—the baby dragged out into a harsh and sterile world of bright lights and sharp sounds. So a distorting process begins, there at the beginning.

A difficult birth does not, in itself, create a difficult life, though it may leave an imprint of vulnerability. The body remembers, even more acutely than the mind. Watch a person reliving their birth.[4] They twist and squirm, their head turning first one way then the other, just as it did on their journey through the birth canal. Then they take a deep shuddering breath. Even as an adult, our physical self will attempt to release the stored energy of a traumatic entry into the world.

My own earliest experiences were advantageous. I was conceived during a second honeymoon on the Spanish island of Majorca, a respite from ongoing marital conflicts. My mother gave birth effortlessly. She told me her waters broke in a local shop, causing the Irish bachelor shopkeeper enormous embarrassment. The birth almost occurred on the stairs as she rushed up to the bedroom and it was assisted by the same midwife who stayed at our house before and after most of her labors. My mother enjoyed the sensuality of infants and I was breast-fed for my first eighteen months of life.

When I contact the sense of my beginning, it is warm, welcoming and easy. I believe, viscerally, even when events contradict that belief, that the world is relatively benign; no one is out to get me. I am grateful for a stable start to my life.

Evaluating a house, we need to know the condition of its foundations, the first things that were built. Does the edifice stand solid and square or will it subside and crack because the support is inadequate? Knowing our own beginning—our conception, birth and earliest experiences—provides a context for understanding our later responses to life. That knowledge gives crucial information about our strengths and vulnerabilities, our typical ways of approaching the demands of living.

When you are in a relaxed and dreamy state, ask yourself these questions: What do I know about my conception and birth? Was I wanted, planned and welcomed? Was labor and delivery easy and natural? Was there a period of separation from my mother? How did she nourish me? Gather information from parents or those who might have inside knowledge about that time. Take time to feel and imagine how it was for that tiny infant.

You may come across a hesitation or resistance in yourself to believing that you could ever re-experience those feelings. There is a gulf of forgetting that has to be crossed. The circumstance of your birth does not supply *the* answer to why you are as you are— it adds another piece to the puzzle of your life, a richer context to who you can become.

The Ancestral Pool

Even if the birth is easy and natural, diving out of the womb we do not plunge into clear and tranquil waters. On the contrary, as C. G. Jung says, we are born into the "unconscious atmosphere" of the family. What is this, our first energetic environment? Using traditional language, let's call it the *ancestral pool*.[5]

Our life is the end point of uncountable generations of predecessors. Each forebearer contributes genetic possibilities but also adds to an unbroken ancestry of processes. Every child in a lineage takes on the unconscious influences of every preceding parent and, if not aware, will pass those on to their own offspring. Multitudes of lives and happenings add to a river of process, flowing from generation to generation. This all surges into a reservoir carried by your parents. The complexity is incomprehensible.

I will use my family as an example. My ancestral pool is filled with the influx of two contrasting parental streams. On my mother's side are generations of despotism and the need to control others. The family owned "satanic mills", woolen factories of degradation and exploitation in nineteenth century Northern England. My grandmother escaped family servitude during the First World War to join the Red Cross and married a middle-aged, slightly unworldly, scholarly barrister. She and her daughter, my mother, were trapped and controlled financially by her family when this man died prematurely.

The Second World War marred my mother's life. Her French fiancé was killed in the first weeks of enemy engagement. Not long after, while recuperating from a sinus operation, her hospital was bombed during the Blitz of London. She awoke under tons of rubble still holding the amputated hand of the nurse she had been talking with moments before. Her cracked skull and swelling brain were only recognized and operated on many months later. By that time she had married my father on a wartime impulse. She never imagined he could survive. Both her parents died when they were sixty. She eventually died of a further head injury when she was sixty.

I see the influence of this maternal torrent more in my siblings than in myself; this may be part of an inherited blindness. There is strong-mindedness, a definite quality to our way of being in the world. There is also a need to control our destiny and a most powerful need *not* to be controlled by others. We are difficult to manage. We avoid being trapped and many of us have escaped to other countries. There is a vein of spirituality. None of us understands war. One of my brothers is a strict Buddhist monk practicing "ahimsa," non-harm to all living beings.

My father's stream of process has a different quality. His great-

great grandfather was a blacksmith who struck it rich during the nineteenth century in Wales. The following generations favored a life of gentrified entitlement on a country estate. Unconscious wastefulness reached a peak with my grandfather. At his death the 22,000-acre estate had dwindled to a mere 2,000 acres. His wife, my grandmother, was a Welsh aristocrat with a deep feeling for the soil. She gardened in the huge estate garden until she died. Into this shielded milieu, my shy and reticent father was born.

After the trauma of English 'public school' and a short period farming in South Africa he joined the Royal Air Force at the beginning of the war. He bombed Germany in air raid after air raid, becoming the single survivor of two squadrons. It is torture to have imagination when you are turning cities into infernos and your friends are being slaughtered all around you.

Just months after my parents married, my mother began to have seizures caused by her head injury. My father could not cope and he simply disappeared for a few months. After the war, hoping for a simpler life, they escaped to a small farm in Ireland. Still nothing worked. After numerous disasters the farm went bankrupt and they returned, poverty stricken, to Wales. The ancestral influences had dragged my father into a financial morass; you cannot run an Irish farm like a gentleman's estate.

From my father's line comes the urgent impulse to garden, to live a country life. Now in his eighties, he tends his myriad of trees, shrubs and plants every day. All my siblings and I are, or have been, talented and compulsive cultivators of the earth. One brother holds world records for giant vegetables. None of us is very talented financially. We still hold some of that aristocratic disdain for money and a sense of being different and unique. There are two kinds of people, Evanses and the rest.

I was born into this whirlpool of turbulent forces. All of it surges in my blood and in my psyche. My parents' processes, especially, are written deep in my soul. Without direct involvement, I am scarred by the craziness of the Second World War. We suppose the tragedies and benighted attitudes of our forebearers are safely in the past, yet their effects live on within us.

The shadow of our ancestors binds and often blinds us. We inherit greed, selfishness and fear as a whole cloth from ancestors who fought to survive, who clutched at what they could hold with all their might. Our society reflects that inheritance. We have the ability and knowledge to cure disease, irradicate hunger, create a harmonious world, yet we do not. With all the remedies and resources available, we still allow many to live in ignorance, poverty and despair. We are still gripped by fear of difference, the paranoia of nationalism, racism and religious bigotry. A modern child is born into a clean, gleaming environment, the ancestral forces swirling, uncontained just below the surface.

Like it or not we are the end product of uncountable generations. Human, humanoid, primate, reptilian, invertebrate ancestors stretch back in an unbroken line to the first life on this planet.[6] Our hubris tells us that somehow we are more important, special, enlightened—beyond and better than those who went before. We pretend we have sprung without antecedents into this world. Maybe our ancestors are incensed by this neglect. The Bible tells us the negative influence, the sins of our fathers extend "unto the seventh generation." Ancestral influences are part of who we are. To ignore them is dangerous.

Often, because we have made an effort to be as unlike our parents as possible, we believe we have shaken off the ancestors. In reality, our antagonism binds us as tightly as compliance. To rebel is to connect through negativity; opposition strengthens its opposite. Because my parents were always separating, one sister struggled to stay married regardless. She endured a difficult relationship far longer than was healthy. We have to be careful to not sustain the worst aspects of ancestral forces by our animosity. These forces require acknowledgment, resolution and integration, not hostility and estrangement.

Your human ancestors were real people just like you and I. Each had their loves, dreams and fears and lived real, vivid, detailed lives; each faced death. You probably have striking similarities of looks, speech and mannerism to some forebearers. If you explore certain deeper layers of yourself, you would meet some interesting characters.

Ancestral detective work is fascinating. One client found out that his great-grandfathers had been involved in a gunfight in which one died and that there was a thread of extreme violence running through the male side of his family. Another confirmed her deep connection with Native American spirituality knowing that an ancestor had survived the Trail of Tears to settle in Oklahoma. Confronting his father to get information about his mother, who died when he was young, a client was told that his maternal grandfather committed suicide. His own father had helped cover up the death for insurance purposes. Another root of his depression and secrecy was exposed.

You are your history and also the history of those who went before you. Some say that before each rebirth we choose the family, the ancestral pool that will provide just the right karmic situation for our spirit. How can you know who you are, and who you are trying to become, if you do not know the context into which you were born? Our ancestors are our burden and our helpers. They are engraven into the layers that encrust our soul. To know them is to know yourself better.

Ask yourself, "What is the quality of my ancestral pool? What was the atmosphere I was born into?" Recall and write down the old family stories and myths that you were told. Ask siblings, parents and relatives what they know and remember. Trace the differences between your maternal and paternal sides and imagine what happened when those became joined. Look up your family tree on the World Wide Web. You never know exactly what you will find but it will give you insight into the forces that drive and sustain you.

Growing Up

Through our whole life we try to achieve a better accommodation to our ancestral inheritance. We meet those ancestors most forcefully through the attitudes and actions of our parents as they dealt with us, their offspring. As someone said to me: "The main task in life is learning to forgive your parents!"

During childhood we are at the mercy of parental ignorance. I have witnessed the damage done to a generation of babies through the misguided ideas of scheduled bottle-feeding. Books advocating this approach gave permission to abandon infants to hunger and isolation. Even without those benighted attitudes, all parents, whatever their intentions, are less than perfect and leave inadvertent scars on their children. Every impulse, sensation and interaction impacts an infant far more intensely than we imagine as adults. A baby's experience is vivid and timeless.

As we age, time changes. The future is shorter than the past, not because there are fewer years but because each year is experienced as a proportion of the whole. At age two, a year is half of your life, each day is endless and a week is inconceivable. At age forty, a year is but a fortieth of your life—a month goes by in a flash and death is not so far away.

Imagine all of the past year's events and experiences compressed into a week. Imagine that they are all new and unknown and never felt before, and you are powerless to influence them. That is what it is to be a newborn. There is more quality and quantity of experience in the first three years of our life than there is in the next thirty. No wonder that psychotherapists are obsessed with childhood.

At age four I realized that adults had no conception of what it was to be a child. They seemed to have developed a total amnesia of their earlier experience. I determined that I would never forget,

I would hold on to that vivid sense of being open, young and filled with vitality. Now I can only capture a hint of that aliveness, like the faint scent of wilted flowers. Layers of experience obscure its freshness as I too have joined the ranks of burdened and compacted adults.

We each had moments in our childhood when we were totally present, engaged fully with our being. I look at my four-year-old daughter, drawn to every new sight, sound and touch, overflowing with curiosity and imagination, loving and hating with vehemence. Life is her playground. What happens to us adults that we forget? I then look at my son, aged eleven and I see the beginnings of the forgetting.

In Rudolf Steiner's developmental system, the tenth year is pivotal.[7] Before that age the child's soul is not completely embodied; imagination and fantasy still hold sway. During the period between eight and ten, the child begins to be drawn fully into the physical, with all its demands, expectations and materiality: "the veil of magic participation slips from the world."[8]

Unlike the turbulence of adolescence, this change is subtle and often unremarkable. In adult psychotherapy, the period between eight and twelve receive least attention, unless trauma occurred.[9] Being left out, teased or bullied at school are the usual complaints; parental divorce is the the most common difficulty. For many, however, those years are uncomplicated. Long summers, vacations, sports and intense friendships make up the high points. It is a time of consolidation before the hormonal storm of adolescence.

Adolescence

I left school at age fifteen. I was working and living away from home by the age of sixteen. This is not the situation of the average US middle-class teenager. In my clinical experience most young people do not reach psychological independence until their late twenties—and still may be financially dependent on parents for many years after. Many males and increasing numbers of females cling to the irresponsibility of youth as long as possible. Modern American adolescence is an extended life period that seldom ends before age twenty-five.

Adolescence is a period of finding yourself, both figuratively and literally. "Who am I supposed to be?" is the first big question. "What should I do with my life?" is the next. Searching for identity we look to see where we fit, which group will accept us. We also push away the primary source of our earlier selves—our parents and all authorities. The internal and inarticulate struggle for identity is a momentous affair for the teenager.

Just before and after puberty there is an upswelling of questions about life and meaning. A doorway opens between the self and the Greater process. Often a sensitive child will have strange experiences, precognitive dreams, and powerful intuitions. More often than not that child is born into a down-to-earth family where that kind of 'nonsense' is not accepted. Even if the family is formally religious, mystical aspirations may be squashed or made fun of at home or by peers. The adolescent will see hypocrisy in the conventional religious practices of the parents, finding it empty and meaningless. In disgust, the adolescent discards the spiritual baby with the religious bath water.

I remember my own inner struggles as a teenager. My sixteen-year-old resolution to the question, "Does life have meaning?" had a certain twisted logic. I argued with myself: "If life has no meaning it is only reasonable to kill myself now, rather than wait to die later. If I do not kill myself it suggests that I believe life does have meaning. So if I do not commit suicide, and I wish to be honest, I should live *as if* life is meaningful." That conclusion carried me through my adolescent depression. It proved its worth over the years.

When Matt told me how he lost his faith at the age of seventeen, I could see he had reached a darker conclusion. He and a friend would get 'high' and discuss the 'meaning of life' late into the night. The more the intellectual talk continued, the more he assumed that there was no purpose, no ultimate reality and no sense to being alive. He embraced a nihilistic form of existential thought, became a critical silent watcher. Religion was puerile nonsense, suicide a rational option.

Many years later his vitality frozen and calcified, he looked out at life from the distance behind his eyes. All that remained was a penetrating mind. Dreams of empty deserts and drowned women helped us slowly dismantle the splits in his being and make room for his heart to feel again. He still looks on formal religion with a jaded eye, is still hesitant to accept too much New Age 'gobbledygook', but he can feel life and wants to be a part of it.

Can you recall the anguish of your own growing identity? Did you feel it or were you too distracted to notice? The irrational desires and emotional intensity of adolescence is something we may wish to forget. Being accepted and acceptable to a peer group, obsession with the changing body and sexual urges, pressure to perform and conform in school, teasing, bullying and isolation are the fabric of many young people's lives. The recent spate of high school massacres, the horrendous suicide rates among teenagers (gay teenagers in particular) evidence a vast reservoir of suffering. We can only understand if we are willing to explore our own suppressed pain rather than look for some political magic bullet.

Finding the Right Relationship

Freud said that the important essentials of an adult life are Love and Work. He was right. These are the Yin and Yang, the receptive and active expressions of our being in the world. Learning to love and finding our true work are the two cornerstones of a complete life. Both require a searching journey into ourselves. We must confront our fears and restrictions, attempt to reach our vision of what is possible while recognizing what is actually available.

We first encounter the beginnings of adult relationship in adolescence, a time of extreme passions, both devotion and antipathy. Our hearts are beginning to be exercised, creating space and discernment to find relationships that will contain and sustain us throughout life. The first task is to satisfy any unmet sensory and contact needs of childhood.

Most teens have a desperate but repressed urge for physical contact—a powerful unmet *touch hunger*. Young girls preen, fidgeting with their face and bodies. Young men are more circumspect. They roughhouse, mock fight, and punch each other on the shoulder. First sexual encounters are mostly an attempt to satisfy this intense desire for intimate sensory stimulation. If a young couple surrender to the hunger, they spend hours twined around each other like vines, feeling and holding. They are doing important work—filling the unmet needs of childhood. If successful, they may be able to choose a companion later in life, freer from unconscious compulsions.

Most adolescent relationships (those under the age of 25 in the United States) are like exercise or practice for the emotional self. The young person is trying to discover who they are through relationship with a valued person. Like any preliminary exercise, there is trial and error, big mistakes and painful disappointments.

I recall a male client who, after a divorce and one extremely dysfunctional liaison, shared the insight that he would probably take at least another two or three attempts before he would be able to get relationship right. The internal and social pressure to find a mate is so great that most give in, accepting whoever is currently available. However, if you dig deep enough you will find an unconscious assumption that out there exists your 'soul mate' also waiting to find you.

I was once involved in a discussion about sex, spirituality and marriage with Sudarto, a funny, wise and uninhibited Indonesian elder.[10] You could never tell if he was making fun of us immature

Western men as we sat in a circle around him and plied him with inane questions. After he spoke he was likely to laugh uproariously, his practically toothless mouth wide open, his big belly shaking beneath the folds of his sarong.

One young man asked him if there was such a thing as a soul mate and how should he find her. Sudarto got very serious as he replied in broken English: "Yes, you have a soul mate but she is hard to find. There is a woman in every half a million who has a soul, a good match with you. Better to look for that one-in-half-a-million than to keep waiting for your true mate. You can be happy with second best." He looked round at the circle of single and earnest men as we hung on every word, and burst into laughter again.

Most do not find their soul mate or even second best. Almost half of all marriages in the United States end in divorce. It is a personal tragedy and an epidemic that affects millions of lives, particularly those of the children. Something is not right and it is easy to become cynical and jaded.

The Hollywood fantasy of a smooth and perfect relationship in which both partners live 'happily ever after' is a seductive trap that foreordains deep disappointment. Who said marriage or relationship should be easy? Like life, it is a creative task that requires the utmost attention and effort. George Bernard Shaw tells us that, "Hell is other people." His words cynically point to the reality that relationship is difficult.

A divorced client came in with a 'big dream.' *She is in her garage when a man in blue overalls pulls up in a truck. He tells her, "I am the Holy Spirit. God sent me in this form because he knows you only believe things that are concrete." After delivering a life changing message, just as he turns to leave he says, "By the way, you know you can have a relationship if you want one." She replies, "But I am too difficult to live with," to which the Holy Spirit responds, "You know, **everyone** is difficult to live with!"*

I am difficult to live with and you are difficult to live with. That is the truth. No person will always agree with your opinions, will be exactly who you want them to be. Relationship requires that we give up part of our freedom, autonomy and preferences. We make a sacrifice of our ego on the altar of love and connection.

Many relationships should never have begun—but some become sacred spaces for the growth of both souls. So what makes for a successful connection?

The more each person's process resonates harmoniously, the more they can create a wide enough relationship to contain all aspects of their being. The couple's outer nature must mesh to some extent; it is easier if they enjoy similar activities and have similar styles of approaching the world. From an inner point of view, the more open and available they are to each other, the stronger their intimacy, sharing and support will be. These are the elements of compatibility, the basics for creating a lasting shared connection.

It is most often in the deeper unconscious processes that things become tangled and dark. Unless each person is able to know and accept him—or herself deeply, with all the shadow aspects, something is liable to jump out and bite. The old unresolved childhood stuff of dependencies, resentments and compulsions will inevitably be expressed and acted out. It is then that love goes on trial, is found guilty and summarily executed.

What do you do when your partner never seems to learn, never comes to terms with his or her issues? The first questions to ask is, "What is my part in this drama? How am I contributing to the situation?"

Do not delude yourself that you are blameless or without responsibility, even if that responsibility is simply to get out quickly and cleanly. There are always two sides to every relationship; both have their merits and shortcomings. A good partnership continues to negotiate a shared reality even when all seems bleak and lost; it does not accept the 'truth' imposed by any one person. This holds true even when a couple sees a marital counselor. The therapist does not know it all, does not have a monopoly on reality. The couple has to discover which world they can agree to live in together.

Shared values and spiritual beliefs are a foundation that can withstand the earthquakes and aftershocks of life. Without solid values and commitment to awareness and mutual change, relationships stagnate or conflict spirals out of control. Many relationships founder on the rocks of fear and spiritual apathy. Neither of the participants can muster enough courage, enthusiasm and energy to do anything before it is too late. There is not enough patience and tenacity to keep love alive.

In a supportive marriage, one partner may shoulder the majority of the spiritual burden, while the other is shrouded in clouds of doubt, disbelief and cynicism. Even in a seemingly hopeless case, I have seen a cold cynic slowly melt beneath the warmth and sincerity of his loving partner. The transcendent is always available, inviting us to participate in a more complete and flowing way of being together.

In the best cases, couples grow to become soul mates though they started far apart. Allowing ourselves to resonate with another person helps reconnect broken pieces and blocked energies. A solid loving relationship contains everything, both light and dark, in each partner; it becomes a vessel for healing and transformation. The spiritual requirements of living a whole life in relationship, of surrendering to love, is the essence of "til death us do part."

Finding the Right Work

Right work, like good relationship, nourishes and stretches. Work is not accomplishment, work is not occupation nor is it a way of making a living. Work is the container for the active, outgoing aspect of our energies. It is anything we do to create and produce a difference in the world.

We are born different in order to make an inimitable impact on the world. Our individual life adds something to all that went before, becomes part of an ecology of being. If we do not fill our own particular niche in life, it is as if a species has become extinct.

The manner each of us has of relating to the world, the way we think, feel, sense and act, will never be duplicated. Each of us has potentials that are incomparable. These are our talents. Formless in themselves, they are intertwined with the whole of our being. Talents are skills, passions, and unique ways of seeing the universe. Individually, our talents may be nothing extraordinary, but in that special combination that is you or I something comes into being that never existed before.

Searching for our right work, we unconsciously look for an outer container for inner talents, what you might call 'vocation.' Sam Keen tells us that vocation is a spiritual call to do something particular in the world.[11] It becomes a channel through which those gifts of our fundamental nature are manifest. Vocation is often associated with 'worthy' occupations that are directly of service to others. Everyone, from the wealthy businessman to the homemaker, may be following their true talent. Parenting is possibly the hardest and most valuable work that any human can do. For many it is a spiritual calling.

Talents do not come with a label. Because the world never perfectly reflects our human need, there is always a struggle to find the right fit between inner aptitude and outer activity. If you are lucky, there is an occupation that is a good enough match. If not, you may have to invent a new undertaking that has never been seen before. Maybe you design a different kind of web site, create a giant sculpture or find a means to use your subtle intuitive ability. Each of these becomes a vocation that mirrors your distinctive talents.

Work that is fitting and reflects your essential nature brings inner satisfaction. If, on the other hand, you merely work to make money, true contentment will never be yours. A software manager told me of his lifelong passion for anthropology. Instead of visiting cultures around the world, he sits in an airless office. A retired teacher I know realized late in life that his talent was and is to be a musician. He had ignored his passion for music and been waylaid by his fear of not making a living. Now he has missed his vocation and it is too late to start over.

It is not always easy to recognize your talent and find your vocation. I once worked in a sales office for a huge packaging conglomerate. I was miserable every minute. I then tried crofting on a tiny farm in remotest Ireland and this proved to be a little better. Then I tried carpentry and building which was much better. Finally, in a quiet state, I received vivid moving pictures as if seen through a telescope backward. In the images I was working like a physician. When people came to see me, I did nothing, yet still they got better.

At the time, it made no sense to me. So I tucked it away in the back of my mind. A few months later, a friend insisted that I read the book, C. G. Jung's *Memories, Dreams and Reflections*. Almost immediately, I knew Jung was describing what I needed to do; I was being directed toward the profession of psychotherapy. Psychotherapy is my vocation as well as my occupation; it is a vehicle that expresses the essence of my talents.

Many people chose to sell their time, energy, and satisfaction for material comfort and security. They give away their lives to the highest bidder. What is the price of your life? Each minute spent working in a job you hate is a minute subtracted from your existence that can never be redeemed. Taken in the context of the long body, it seems crazy to waste one third of our short lifespan on activity that has no meaning.

Are you ignoring your talents? Are you afraid to follow your dream, your "bliss" as Joseph Campbell calls it? If you have to be an artist, no matter how impractical, when will you put paint to canvas? If you are an entrepreneur, when will you start to raise the capital? Not quite realizing worldly success will seldom be an issue if you are following your passion. You will certainly regret never having tried. Working at a vocation, the manifestation of our true talents, enriches our whole being.

The Risk of Life

With age, we grow increasing independent. No longer a helpless child, we learn skills and abilities to get what we need from the world. This is what we mean by the term adult—a person who has achieved an effective relationship with the world.

With maturity we hope to achieve inner growth that helps us become more emotionally stable and secure. But that is not always so. Many 'successful' people are only adult on the outside. They have not achieved internal coherence; their self remains immature. Without inner integration, there is no true individuality. The person is not whole—not a working system. You might say they are a collection of parts looking for coherence.

Without this inner coherence we are at the mercy of conflicting forces: the need for security versus the need for expansion. We wish to remain safe and secure but we still have to go out into the dangerous world each day. Our 'survival instinct' prompts us to avoid danger yet we long for adventure and new experiences. Caught in this dilemma between safety and risk, we become immobilized.

The timid young man afraid to go out on a date is caught in this struggle. He wants relationship but cannot face the thought of devastating humiliation or rejection. The successful businesswoman who hates her job but cannot give up her benefits is similarly trapped. Something in her knows that she is slowly dying from inertia and boredom, but it is safer to stay stuck than to take the risk of leaving. Only when a person can begin to face and embrace the essential insecurity of life does the trap dissolve.

Much of the work of therapy is invoking courage. Fear binds us, keeps us small. Curiosity, interest, love and even anger are inner forces that engage with life more fully. I am always happy when the timid client finally blurts out, "I'm fed up being like this. Something's got to change, no matter what I have to do." Her frustration blasts through anxiety and hesitation like a rocket defying gravity. This is part of the training of life. She has to learn to face reality as fully as possible and not back down. Like each of us, she will eventually be put to the final test—facing her own dying.

There is ultimately no safety. Our material form inevitably yields to the forces of un-life. The entropic principle, disorganization and disintegration, holds sway over the physical. Eventually our body succumbs and we die. We can never be fully prepared for that terminal event. But we can have gathered enough inner strength to meet death with dignity and curiosity.

Death

Humans do not really believe in personal extinction. Ask yourself, "Will I cease to exist when I die?" Whatever your conscious ideas, regardless of whether you are religious or atheist, if you look deep enough inside yourself, you will find a place that assumes everlastingness. Our unconscious does not entertain non-existence; we live each day with an implicit assumption of immortality. So, assuming that our life process does not totally cease, it must transform into something else.

When I was fourteen I almost died in a boating accident with my brother and father: *The wind was brisk from the open sea and the tide was taking us out against the wind at a fair rate. We rounded a point and noticed the line of waves stretching from the far side of a semi-circular bay—a giant wall of white-tops, standing in our path. So we headed toward shore, but the tide was insistent. The wall kept getting closer, now at the rear of the boat. Then it struck and without warning we were turned turtle—scrabbling out, clinging to the upturned boat*

113

and riding out the rough seas.

Time slowed. I felt warmed and drifty. My brother struck out after his floating bag of clothes so I collected him, noticed the flecks of foam at the corner of his mouth. Yet the feeling remained. My Father let off our last hope, a red smoke canister and we waited.

The warmth seeped into my bones and my thoughts. We were dying—and that was OK. I pictured my sisters with a kind of sweet sadness to realize how they would grieve at our deaths. It was the ones left behind that would feel the pain—it would be their tragedy, not ours. I felt a kind of relief, a letting go and relaxing into the soft welcoming state; it was all over. The life-jacket kept me buoyant in the water but couldn't stop me slipping away.

The imperative to live is powerful. I have a vivid image of my younger brother scooting up a rope ladder slung over the towering black side of the German ship; moments previously he had been comatose. At the moment of our rescue, even though I felt so calm and complete inside, there was nothing that could have kept me in the water.

Like the vast majority of people with 'near death' experiences, I am left with an unshakable conviction that there is no end to life. I have an irrational conviction of personal continuity, that the essential me will continue in a different form. Death is merely a transition into another state of being.

Whether our unique individual pattern dissipates with death or continues transformed, is the recurring question of religion. As the physical body undergoes metamorphosis, the essential energetic process is not necessarily lost. At any moment in our body thousands of cells are dying, yet we remain ourselves. Our whole being is not totally dependent on our physical parts.

When a string of an instrument is played, other strings resonate in harmony. If the original string is damped, the resonance endures. We are vibrations of life; maybe the pattern of that vibration reverberates beyond our death, a ripple in the universal flux.

Life seeks ways to transmit the precious gift of life. In its battle against entropy the Life Force deploys its weapons of transformation and reproduction. At the very least our creations live on after us, carrying an energy signature into the future. There is something of me in this book, in the house I have built, in the clients I have helped. Certainly my genes endure in my children. Life is tenacious and extravagant in propagating offspring. Always, in many different forms, living processes endeavor to beget other living processes.

Embracing the Thread of Life

The future is limitless possibility constricted by the narrow lens of the present. We are always dying and in the long body we already exist at our deathbed. Can we experience the wholeness of our life, live in this moment that is the apex of both past and future? Can we live with the reality of our frailty and mortality, yet maintain a sense of optimism and tranquillity? It is a wonderful, dangerous business being alive.

I have a practice that I call "life inoculation." I let myself think, in detail, about the most devastating events that could happen. My wife and children could be kidnapped or murdered. My house could burn down. I could be paralyzed or brain damaged in a car accident. Then I let myself imagine my reaction and how my life would change. I keep asking myself, "Would something essential within me be able to survive those traumas? Would I lose my sense of myself, my belief in the meaningfulness of life? Could I still find joy?"

This is a scary practice. It walks the tightrope of anxiety and flirts with depression. I also find it enlivening and comforting. It strengthens my resolve to live the most fully now, this moment, when everything is comparatively marvelous. I feel gratitude for simply being.

To be human is to be showered with priceless gifts. Our bodies are miraculously designed to act on and in the world, to heal and keep us alive. Our minds are amazing organs of awareness and experimentation. We can mentally take apart the clockwork of life to see its mechanisms, project its possibilities into the future and analyze the results. To balance our overactive minds we have our hearts with their ability to feel and connect—to put back together what has been taken apart.

We have to care for these gifts, make the most of our human capacities. Bodies need stimulation, activity, good nourishment, a balance of exercise and relaxation. Hearts demand that we become better 'lovers'—feel and know the essential and meaningful connection between all things, all people, and all possibilities of experience.[12] Minds, too, need exercise, the exertion of deep thought that takes nothing for granted.

I remember as an undergraduate immersing myself in a project on the nature of consciousness. I was tenacious and obsessed. For weeks I kept those formless and slippery ideas turning in my mind, so vigorously that I could feel my head flushed and overheated with the flow of blood. When the project was complete, my mind was clear for the first time. I pushed back the fuzzy barrier that kept me unfocused.

Body, heart and mind are meant to work together with different abilities complementing and adding to each other. Their purpose is to allow us to experience the whole of our lives. To paraphrase Socrates, *the unexperienced life is not yet lived*.[13] We know our lives as meaningful only as much as we are willing to experience it fully and completely.

We are more than we seem, more than we realize. Knowing the long body of our lives—the passions and pain, the ease and restrictions—we get to know ourselves better. We begin to embrace the whole of life and the destiny it offers.

CHAPTER 6

Vulnerability and Resilience

Life only demands from you the strength you possess.
Only one feat is possible—not to have run away.
—Dag Hammarskjöld

I have two children, a boy and a girl. One is dominant, aggressive, always active and on the go, loving bright colors, new friends and physical stimulation. The other is quiet, intellectual, socially shy, loves classical music and being at home. They are opposites in their approach to life, in the kind of energy they bring to a situation. Contrary to sexual stereotypes it is my four-year-old daughter who is outgoing and my eleven-year-old son who is retiring.

After living with my sensitive son for seven years it was a shock to have to contend with a petite dynamo intent on imposing her will on the world. When they rough and tumble it is my son who is likely to get hurt. Whatever he finds disturbing is exciting fun for her. They live in different worlds of experience, see the same event from different angles. How did they come to be so dissimilar? What subtle combination of genes and experience set them on their divergent ways of being?

Parents know that each one of their children is born unique. A mother naturally sees the spark of individuality in her tiny

117

infant. From the moment of conception every human being manifests an inimitable way of being. We are born into the world with our own nature, the germinal process of our individuality. In technical terms this is our *constitution* and *temperament*.

Constitution and Temperament

Constitution is our physical nature, a tendency to develop a certain bodily type, a particular quality of health and vitality. Embedded in our constitution are our inherent physical strengths and weaknesses. Some families carry a high risk for cancers, baldness, heart disease—others experience robust health into late old age. You may be predisposed to put on weight just by smelling a hamburger. Generations of starving ancestors programmed your body to store energy whenever possible. Yet your friend can eat anything without consequence. Constitutional vulnerabilities are not distributed fairly.

Temperament is more subtle; it is the genesis of our personality and way of being in the world.[1] Some babies are born more sensitive, more intense and more inclined to respond anxiously. Others are compliant, relaxed and placid. Some seem to enjoy an innate rhythm; they eat, nap, and excrete to an internal routine. Others take years to sleep through the night, get potty trained or eat at mealtimes. Many parents, myself included, are shocked to find a later child much less easy to settle and manage than the first.

These inherent differences of constitution and temperament set the scene for the drama of each life. How you look, how you initially respond and behave have enormous impact on the quality of your experience. Every family and society elevates some attributes and stigmatizes others.

The cute little girl who grows to be a stunning woman enjoys exceptional social opportunities. The physically coordinated, white youth who becomes a school athlete is guaranteed special attention.

At the opposite end is the plump boy in a skinny family who stands out and becomes the brunt of comments and jokes that reinforce his shyness. The adolescent with scarlet acne or a speech impediment, the fat girl with glasses, the sensitive gay boy, black kids in an intolerant white school—all these will experience the misery of being different.

Many believe genetics cause all the differences between individuals. This is a dangerous simplification. Having certain genes does not mean we are predestined to become a certain kind of person with a certain kind of life. Genes carry nothing but information—they must have an environment to be realized in the world. It is environment and its interaction with innate potentials that produces individual differences. You cannot separate a seed from the ground in which it grows.[2]

We come into being through the connection between our nature and our experience. This interaction is the genesis of our individual process. It creates that delicate balance of weakness and strength—our *vulnerability* and *resilience*.[3]

Like the long body in the last chapter, imagine a whole life process as a winding rope of many intertwined strands. Certain of those strands are incomplete, brittle, broken, weak or unraveled. Those are our vulnerabilities. If the rope is stressed, those strands will part, putting strain on others. Eventually, with increased tension, the rope snaps at that point. Then we contract a disease or break down emotionally.

With no stress, those ragged spots go unnoticed; there is enough strength in the connection between other strands to hold everything together. Resilience is the elasticity, the very interconnection that buffers and protects the weaker strands. It allows the rope to twist and bend, to conform to distorting forces without suffering irreparable damage. We cope with life.

Constitution and Health

Each of us has particular frailties; each has strengths. Our physical constitution may be sturdy, defying illness, healing quickly. Or it may be more fragile, reacting to any noxious experience or substance. Do you know your own constitutional weaknesses and strengths? Maybe you are prone to digestive troubles or migraines when life gets too stressful. Maybe you get agitated and forgetful. Or possibly, you take your health and vitality for granted because it's always been fine—your immune system stays robust.

We rely on our immune system to keep us healthy. Whenever an immune system goes out of balance, illness results. If our immune system overreacts to external intruders, we develop allergies; if it does not respond vigorously enough, we develop infections. If the immune system does not recognize cellular distortions, cancers have the opportunity to spread. If it reacts too harshly certain parts of our body get harmed; autoimmune diseases, such as multiple sclerosis or rheumatoid arthritis, result. Each immune system has its particular vulnerabilities, its specific disharmony. As with all human processes, any imbalance in our system causes illness and suffering.

Our modern world, with its toxic chemicals and even more toxic stresses, creates its own diseases. Unlike the epidemics of the past, the causes of some modern illnesses are harder to pin down. Global allergies, cancers, autoimmune diseases, chronic fatigue and yeast infestation seem to have their inception in the interplay between noxious substances and individual vulnerability. This vulnerability often exists in the relationship between psyche and body.

I see clients who come to therapy because of lost concentration, anxiety and depression associated with non-specific illness. Their vitality and resilience are depleted, yet they function in the world. These individuals, both male and female, often drive themselves to the point of collapse. Their childhood experiences of neglect or abuse pass on an agitated inner tension compelling them to overactivity. As a result, their whole system collapses in retaliation; at least then they are forced to rest. It takes a lifestyle change and much inner work for their resilience to reassert itself.

One man, John, was involved in various nefarious and illegal activities as a young man. When he came to me he was still hounded by terrifying dreams of men with guns and police busts. His anxiety was intense and incapacitating; it exactly mirrored his physical state of debilitating dizziness and chronic diarrhea. For the longest time he equated his bouts of panic with allergic reactions. Medical intervention got his systemic fungal infection under control, but it took working through his childhood losses and trauma before he could relax and be healthy.

Vulnerability

At least John had the ability to influence his life experience. Those whose systems are compromised by genetic or prenatal disturbances may never have that choice. Some are born with inherent damage that is beyond their capacity to heal. Cystic fibrosis is one such instance.

I first saw Sharon when she was seventeen. Pale, with a transparent, fragile beauty, she was already preparing for her inevitable death. Her whole life had been one of drugs, special diet and daily physical therapy poundings to clear her lungs. She had never known anything different from the moment she was diagnosed as a cystic fibrosis baby. A few years later she got pregnant and had to have an abortion against her will. The baby would have killed her. When I saw her last she was doing surprisingly well on new medication—but she knew her life would be short and circumscribed.

Childhood autism is another example of profound vulnerability. Often associated with mental disability, the autistic child may never join the world of human relationship. Michael, an adolescent I saw as an intern could not connect. He remained trapped and alone in a world of objects. His eyes would slide over my face. I was no different to him than the chair he sat in, just another thing in his visual field. His behavior was repetitive, ritualized and compulsive—screaming, pacing and rocking, his fingers moving restlessly in front of his eyes.

This quality of repetition and drivenness shows us what happens when we do not develop—we get stuck in repetitive, meaningless cycles. When we cut ourselves off from the flow of life, when we retreat from love and contact, we become 'autistic,' caught in a stagnant pattern of being. We have the choice to recognize our disconnection and do something about it. Most autistic children do not.

Michael will never take an ordinary role in society. He entered this world with some damage that makes it impossible for him to survive unaided. As if that was not enough, at the age of five he experienced multiple losses. When his parents divorced, his mother gave him up to an agency—she could not cope. In his susceptible state, we will never know how this affected him. We do know, from decades of research and our own personal experience, that the impact of parental behavior on a child is hard to overestimate.

The Vulnerable Family

Parents channel early development. They are containers for the child's earliest experience. Birthing a child is an event in their life to which parents react in their own particular, and sometimes peculiar, way. Each parent has his and her own ideas and prejudices of what it is to bring up a child in the 'right' manner. How to hold, feed, change and relate to that infant is often preprogrammed by family tradition—the influence of the ancestors asserting itself.

All this attention is focused onto the fragile process that is a new human being. If the couple know how to be together, how to connect to the baby naturally through predictable routines and rituals, comfort and cuddles, the baby will thrive. This is "good enough mothering"—a "holding environment" that does not allow the baby to drop into terror or despair.[4] If it is not good enough—abusive, neglectful, deficient, rigid, unpredictable— then that vulnerable little being will be harmed.

The nature of a child may complement his or her family or it may not. Many come to psychotherapy because they were born 'sensitive' into an average insensitive family.[5] Throughout childhood they were told to get on with it, stop crying and complaining, stop overreacting: "what is all the fuss about?" Constantly misunderstood, their experience discounted, they did not fit the family profile. Other siblings adapted and seemed to thrive, but the 'sensitive' one was always the odd-man-out— feeling more poignantly, thinking more deeply. And when the painful challenges of life occurred, there was no one there to understand.

When life hurts, we have a simple basic need. Consider my young daughter when she falls and scrapes herself. She cries and seeks out the nearest parent. If we can be present with her distress, soothing and reassuring, in a short time she stops crying, pushes us away and gets back to her play. If we are less than available, she begins to whine and cling.

She is trying to get what we all need to heal the pain and anguish—*a safe, containing, attentive connection.* Each child draws inner strength and resilience from a parent or person who is energetically present and not distracted. The natural flow of process, when it is disrupted by trauma, requires an injection of loving support. This is a simple but easily forgotten truth.

Most of our childhood vulnerabilities arise, not simply from adverse experiences but from parental ignorance. I use *ignorance*, not pejoratively, but in the sense of ignoring, avoiding or denying particular aspects of reality. Most parents, myself included, are well-meaning. We love our children to the best of our ability and do for them what we think is right and proper. But we are all blinded by ancestral forces and our own unresolved, tangled issues. Without meaning to we burden our children with our own difficulties.

It is easy to blame all psychological difficulties on poor parenting. The reality is more complex. To be the right parent for every child is almost impossible. It requires unwavering awareness, constant loving attention and an understanding of each child's unique changing needs. A child's nature interweaves with that of the family, the ancestral forces, the family conventions, and the parental expectations. The resulting personality is unexpected and surprising. All parents ask themselves at some time, "Where did this child come from?"

Most of us love and care for our children. We do the best we can within our limitations. But in some families there is not enough energy, attention or love to go around. The child is maltreated and abandoned to his or her own fate. Life quickly becomes a traumatizing disaster.

Trauma

Trauma is anything that leaves an enduring scar, an increased vulnerability in the life process.[6] Yet it is not simply some horrible happening that damages us. Trauma is a process extending in time that jeopardizes our ability to heal and become whole.

Imagine you fall and hurt your knee. If the fall is severe, that knee may never heal completely. If there was previous damage, even if the fall is not bad, the knee will be weakened. What if the fall was minor but the medical attention was incomplete or incompetent? Then again the healing is compromised.

In each of those circumstances the knee was traumatized and the natural health of that limb was not restored completely. Hence, it remained vulnerable. Trauma always has three intertwined aspects: *a noxious event, the impact that event has on a specific individual and the way the environment responds.*

For example, two families go through divorce. In one family the only child is five years old, asthmatic, anxiously attached to the parents. Her grandmother died last year. After the split, the father disappears from the scene and the mother becomes depressed and bitter. That child is severely traumatized.

In the other family there are two children, seven and ten years old. The parents explain to the children why they are separating, the father remains in contact and the parents go to counseling to work through their sadness and resentment. These children are not as traumatized.

Superficially similar events have totally different meanings and impacts. To understand trauma we have to know that each person experiences the same event differently, depending on that person's balance of vulnerability and resilience. What is a debilitating shock for one may be a strengthening encounter to another.

I am reminded of a woman client overwhelmed by a Halloween trick; her sister, with ghastly mask, leapt out from behind a corner shouting, "BOO!!" The client nearly jumped out of her skin and remained disembodied and dissociated for weeks. That was a trauma, a disruption in her life process. It hooked into other similar scary and unpredictable events from her childhood, activating a profound vulnerability.

On the other hand, I visited a young man who was paralyzed from the waist down after a motorcycle accident. He refused to give in to bitterness and despondency. Each day was a new opportunity to learn and do more. His body may have been broken but his spirit was not. It was enlivening to be with him, just as it was to be with Kathy, though she was dying a horribly painful death from cancer. Her presence was bright and clear. She would hint at extraordinary inner experiences that left her filled with peace and a deep acceptance. Neither of these people was traumatized by what happened to them. They were able to find the strength, the resilience to face whatever life would bring.

So what did they have in common? They both had loving, caring families and a willingness to face the depths of their experience. In some ways these attributes are two sides of the same coin. Families that are able to love but not smother—to respond appropriately to emotional needs—these families create resilience. A traumatic event resolves when the injured party is surrounded by love and understanding. A loving family is a bottomless treasure.

Abuse

Some people are not so lucky as they seem born to a sinister fate. From conception, life keeps pounding on them until they are almost ready to give in.

There is a world of difference between a single traumatic event and long periods of intractable, unavoidable disturbing experiences. Compare a single incident of molestation by a stranger with years of sexual abuse by a father. Contrast a single bout of sickness with a life-long neurological disease. Consider the death of a friend versus death of a mother. The longer a disturbance continues, the more global its influence on a life, the more likely it is to become woven into the ongoing strands of process. It becomes part of a horrible, taken-for-granted normality.

I have heard too many stories of severe abuse, most banal but some of strange rituals and torture. I hesitate to disclose the full horror of what human beings do to the weak and vulnerable, to their fragile and innocent offspring. The details disgust and sicken. Whatever can be imagined in our worst nightmares, the most lurid horror movie, has happened and may be happening to someone right now.

Too many women and men have been sexually abused. We have no exact figures for those in this culture who are subjected to undesirable and intrusive sexual experiences, but it is endemic. The actuality is hidden behind closed doors, forgotten in some lost memory. Sexual abuse comes in all forms and leaves private and secret scars.

For one woman it might mean a certain bodily sense, without any images, that someone, maybe a grandfather, stroked and stimulated her. It was gentle, confusing, arousing but also disturbing. Because the little girl could not understand it and was not ready for those feelings, it left an uneasiness in her body and its responses. Now she cannot reach satisfying orgasm with her partner.

For another woman it may be the graphic and vivid memory of being raped by her father, while he screamed at her. Her body is still wracked with pains. She fluctuates through cycles of deep depression and panic; dark wells of pollution fill her. It does not help that her father was drunk or that he had somehow confused her with the mother whom he hated.

Both of these women become numbers in a sexual abuse statistic. Their different personal struggles and successes submerged and unrecognized. It helps little to be sympathetic with them as generalized victims of abuse. It helps more to understand the depths and particulars of their own individual experience.

I have wondered for a long time why sexual abuse is so devastating. My answers are still tentative. Sex, like love, partakes of the Life Force. Sexuality spans all levels of process and all aspect of our being. It is physical and organismic—it is transcendent and spiritual—and it is everything in between. When our natural relationship to sex is disturbed by intrusive energies, everything is disturbed.

Like an avalanche that fills the river of life with debris and pollution, sexual abuse blocks, diverts and muddies the flow of the Life Force in a person's being. Everything gets split up and disconnected. Bodily sensations and vitality become distorted, the sense of self confused, relationship with others and the Greater process are disturbed. It is hard to trust yourself, the universe and even God, when the very energy of life has been defiled. Sexual abuse is a betrayal of life itself.

In abusive families, traumatic events are common and there is seldom any caring attention to heal the damage. One parent, usually the mother, may be totally oblivious to the behavior of the other. Or she may have been told by her daughter but is determined to remain ignorant. Both father and mother are complicit in the abuse. Most of these parents have been born into ghastly and bewildering ancestral atmospheres, with traumatizing experiences of their own. Pain and suffering are passed on, as whole cloth, to the children and so the cycle continues.

These children are more than victims of traumatic abuse. They are left, abandoned in a bleak world, to heal themselves with no medicine available. What is amazing is the creativity, resilience and inner strength that they find to live through impossible situations.

The outcome of trauma is hard to predict It depends on too many variables. The age of the child, their birth order in the family, their inherent resilience and the nature of the events each affect the outcome differently. What is most important is whether there were caring people around who could listen and understand. A kind neighbor or sympathetic teacher can do much to repair the worst affects of trauma. Love, from anywhere, is the most potent medicine. Within every person there is a part that never gives up hope completely, that keeps searching for whatever fosters healing.

Dormant Vulnerabilities

With extreme ongoing trauma, a person becomes raw to life, ever ready to be thrown off balance by its stresses. Constantly 'triggered' into crisis by everyday events, our sense of identity becomes unstable. For most of us, vulnerabilities remain dormant. We are relatively secure, only somewhat neurotic. We have managed to successfully adjust to our frailties through a process of compensation.[7]

Like a callus over a wound, a person develops protective patterns that work in the world. This is not pathology per se, but adoption of a life stance that accepts certain restrictions of experience as normal and necessary. Maybe I had a bad meal in a Chinese restaurant once, so now I never eat Chinese food. Or I smoke cigarettes because it helps me relax, and rationalize that it is better than getting fat from overeating. On the surface, these look like minor idiosyncrasies that are not too problematic and other people accept them as part of my personality. However, these areas of inflexibility can suddenly erupt if life shifts dramatically.

The overachieving executive, the 'supermom', the fanatic jogger, the impeccable socialite, each presents a good face to the world. Yet beneath the surface hidden vulnerabilities may be lurking. Successful people are often taken in by their own success, they believe they are healthy. Then crisis strikes, an unexpected loss, an accident, a period of stress and the vulnerabilities surface full-blown. The executive gets suicidal when he is "downsized", the mom falls into a depression as her children leave, the jogger has to confront her distorted body image when she stops exercising, the socialite is filled with emptiness when alone. Their 'perfect' lives have been a cover for hidden distress.

In an otherwise ordinary life, a man may go into a debilitating depression after a relatively minor event such as the dog dying. This is not some random physiological event as some medics would have us believe. This is the end result of a whole train of unresolved losses that have never been dealt with. If you look into his history you find that he never grieved the accidental death of his brother or he bounced from one relationship to another at the merest hint of rejection. He may have been functioning in the world but his inner process was immature in the face of life's demands.

Which uncomfortable parts of your experience do you ignore?

Are you troubled by certain situations—groups of people, flying in an airplane, sexual intimacy? The more you ignore or avoid these signs of vulnerability, the more they restrict your experience and the less resilient you will be when life throws you a curve ball.

The unpredictability of life constantly confronts us with challenges. Any rigidity or inflexibility becomes the greatest point of weakness. Under pressure, a blade of living grass bends while a brittle, dry stick snaps.

Life Turbulence

Unexpected and precipitous change challenges our resilience. Like river rapids and waterfalls, the flow of process seethes and churns. Turbulence is caused by sudden changes in terrain, constricting narrows, huge boulders, sharp drops.[8] These are the crises, the unavoidable life events that beset us on our life journey.

We do not welcome crisis. From a worldly viewpoint there is no benefit or sense in being thrown into inner and outer chaos. Yet from certain kinds of chaos innovative responses emerge.[9] Frederick Flach in his book, *Resilience*, writes about these periods of disruption. He says that crises create *bifurcation points*, periods of change whose outcome are unpredictable. As long as we live, these disruptions are unavoidable.

I came to realize that significantly stressful events, by their very nature, must shake us up and often disrupt the structure of the world around us as well. Moreover, such turbulence has to be accompanied by distress, which can range from mild unhappiness, anxiety or impatience all the way to a state of profound anguish in which we might seriously question who and what we are and the nature of the personal worlds we inhabit.[10]

A solid and placid fireman came to me for a consultation. In the last year his father had died, he had a slight heart attack and his son was nearly ejected from school for smoking marijuana. Work was increasingly stressful. Each call to a fire reminded him that someone was in mortal danger. His dreams were filled with smoldering car wrecks and images of blackened children pulled from the flames. He was overwhelmed, beginning to close down and lose contact with friends and family. His thoughts turned to suicide.

The fireman was more than normally resilient. He prided himself on his physical fitness, his ability to respond to an emergency and the respect he got from colleagues and community. Yet he was being dragged under. As we worked through some of the terrible events he had witnessed, he began to see things in a different light. Maybe he could spend more time relaxing at home, begin to plan for vacations and an early retirement. He began to see his depression as an opportunity to change his life.

Our reactions to life crises differ according to our balance of vulnerability and resilience. For some, the threshold is high. It takes extreme events to trigger distress like those of the fireman. For others, the threshold is swamped by any and all happenings.

Almost every session, Pat would come in with another crisis. One day it was a fight with her sister, another time someone at work had spoken sharply. Even entering a grocery store was an extreme stress that left her shaking and nauseous. Her whole life was filled with terror and threat, reliving the unpredictable rages of her mother. Her experience was a raw and suppurating wound, her life lived on the edge staggering from one emergency to another. She struggled to transform inner confusion and fear into determination.

When life overwhelms us, when it loses its predictability, our inner process becomes filled with turmoil and we get distressed and disoriented. Attempting to relieve the distress, we turn to old and outmoded responses that served to compensate for earlier vulnerabilities. So the fireman 'pulled himself together', put a brave face on it, buckled down to what was expected of him. Pat rushed home, hid in her bedroom, and stuffed herself with any edibles around. Rather than solutions, these coping responses become part of the problem. What is really needed is something different that creates a positive difference.

Any turbulent experience, including illness or accidents, is liable to shake loose an unresolved vulnerability. Many clients begin to remember traumatic childhood incidents only after a car accident. There is something about being 'rear-ended' in a car with the resultant whiplash injury that can throw all compensations into chaos.

Even a fall may have devastating effects. One woman I worked with, Jan, had one accident after another. We tracked the pattern all the way back through sports injuries, headlong dives into basements, slips on ice to an incident at the age of three. She had been playing around the half-built foundations of a house with her older brother. Somehow she fell (or was she pushed?) six feet head first into the concrete basement. Her brother hauled her out, earning gratitude and praise. What was that feeling of being pushed and how could she make sense of it? This was the unanswered question.

Crisis and Opportunity

So why did Jan keep falling? Why do particular events keep triggering crises? The answer is in the deeper process, far from the logic of our conscious mind. The deeper process is in pursuit of integration and wholeness. It does not tolerate loose ends, unresolved memories, and frayed vulnerabilities. Ever on the lookout for opportunities for healing, it uses any suitable situation to push its agenda to the fore.

In every crisis exists a possibility for a new way of experiencing. Our deeper self wants something different to happen so that which is fragmented can reconnect. However, like a recurring dream, that deeper realm is restricted in the ways it talks to us. It sends the same message in similar packaging, just like the one we ignored last time. So the meaning goes unrecognized again.

In many cases, the opportunity for change is missed. Instead of gaining in wholeness, our vulnerabilities are reinforced rather than resolved. The woman, abused as a child, who marries an abuser, is flirting with a dangerous opportunity hoping unconsciously for a healing outcome. The danger often overwhelms the opportunity and more damage results.

Coincidence and Synchronicity

Properly digested, all experience can be nourishing. Hassles and stresses of life are given to us to increase our resilience. Outer events have a habit of reflecting just exactly what is happening deeper within. There is a strange resonance between our deepest needs and the events of the outer world. We wonder about coincidences, whether something is orchestrating things to fit a secret agenda. Is there a conspiracy to make us learn what we need?

C. G. Jung struggled with this question. He came to believe that there is a relational bridge between the different worlds that we inhabit. This relationship he called *synchronicity*. Synchronicity is defined as a physically acausal but a temporally synchronized pattern of connection between inner and outer events.[11] Certain meaningful things happen simultaneously that are not related in a normal physical way.

I think of a person just as the phone rings and he or she is on the line. Or I am talking to a client about their childhood sadness just as a baby cries outside the window. Or, in the world of science and technology, the same discoveries are made completely independently at the same time. I would not be surprised if some other person is, at this moment, writing down exactly these same ideas.

Some dismiss all this as nothing but coincidence. They see the world and their own experience as a collection of random events. This not only ignores observable facts but also avoids an intense involvement in a universe filled with meaning. We are bound to a seamless web of interconnections, of which we recognize only a tiny portion. When synchronicity calls us to attention, we had best take notice.

For certain people, and for most of us at some time, the veil that separates the different worlds is extremely thin. It is as if dreams splash themselves across the canvas of our outer lives.

How do you explain the young woman whose automobile was rear-ended four times in a period of three years? The abuse of her cars and her body stopped when she resolved the sexual abuse by her uncle. What about the man struggling in therapy with his feelings for his angry and intrusive mother? Who moves in next door but a woman who is his mother's spitting image. What about Jillian who dreamed constantly of bears only to meet a grizzly face to face on a hike in Yellowstone.[12]

Many synchronistic events seem banal in the recounting. Yet the person involved cannot avoid the certainty that something numinous is pursuing them. There is no getting away.

Our suffering and tribulations are of little import in the life of the Spirit. There comes a point when we need to see the bigger picture, grasp what life is asking of us. Then everything unexpectedly changes.

One woman took to her bed for a year of depression and physical pain, only to rise renewed, to forge a career as a leader of transformational seminars. A business executive and sufferer of chronic fatigue turned a corner to become a minister to a small parochial congregation. A young mother battled through cancer, divorce and despair, returned to school and found her vocation as a teacher of special education. These people are not extraordinary. They met the challenge of life, faced their own fears and recognized that something more and different was calling them.

'Suffering on purpose' burnishes a space for brighter experience and awareness, a shining mirror in which we see ourselves reflected. Powerful experience creates sturdy resilience.

Each life challenge that is successfully resolved or mastered becomes a source of further strength. Aligning with a greater purpose than our selfish expectations and desires, something unexpected and more expansive will always happen. We do not realize the depth and strength of our own resilience until it is tested.

Resilience

We are born with a measure of resilience that is not fixed. Throughout life, experience weakens or strengthens us. Love and connection is the most fertile soil for vigorous growth of the soul. As we become more whole, more connected to the universe and ourselves, we grow stronger.[13] The depth and quality of that connection determines how creatively we respond to the demands of life.[14]

Many small caring experiences strengthen our being. Even in a less than optimal family, other people who respond to our uniqueness fill in the gaps of unmet needs. The quality of being seen and recognized as a special person is essential. In my own case there was a nun, Mother Columba, who became my surrogate mother at the convent preschool. Her lap was a place of safety and comfort. I was told later that she got into trouble with her superiors for allowing me to nuzzle up to her wimpled breast.

As we grow older, positive experiences taken in and metabolized become an enduring source of inner stability and mastery. Psychologists call this sense of agency *internal locus of control*.[15] This is the conviction that, to a great extent, we control our own destiny, that our fate is not determined by chance or outside forces. We learn this through meeting each challenge of life and seeing it through to a successful conclusion. Like a self-fulfilling prophecy, a strong sense of agency and control produces the success that feeds itself.

I am grateful for my own resilience. I was born constitutionally strong into a large, conflicted and chaotic family. Even with an early childhood trauma (a long hospitalization at age three), there were enough reparative elements to bolster that resilience. My mother loved infants and breast-feeding. My father cared deeply for his children as they became older. Ever-present siblings to fight and play with, a calm and solid grandmother and dedicated teachers, these were enough to hold my fraying self together when it all became too much.

As I look back at my life, I see the periods of fear and retraction that weakened me and the mastered challenges that made me stronger. Now, I am more able to discern the overall pattern, the ways in which I was shaped and formed by experiences and how some of my vulnerabilities transformed to resilience.

As a psychology intern, I was petrified of groups. My first group experience was of a community meeting of fifty psychotic patients and a handful of silent professionals—total terror! Curious about my own fear, I asked myself, "Why should a few people in a room cause me to freeze?" So I plunged into every group situation I could find, read everything I could get my hands on. Eventually, after many years, I was teaching group dynamics.

What challenges have you overcome? Can you reconstruct the pattern of your life to see how much you have achieved, how far you have come on your journey? It is nourishing to celebrate successes, to take in the satisfaction of a job well done or an obstacle surmounted, to recognize your growing resilience.

Creating Resilience

We all need to become more resilient. Unfortunately, there is no simple recipe. What works for me may be totally wrong for you. Yet in therapeutic work there do seem to be some universal rules of thumb.

Therapy aims to transform vulnerability into resilience through resolving stuck experiences. With each client, I explore the obvious insults to the Life Force. Trauma, emotional deprivation and losses are the most common. When a client tells me of a powerful life event and I sense the locked up emotional energy or notice that the thread of life is frayed at that point, I try to help recreate the flowing continuity of identity and experience. With trauma, a disrupted process must be made whole, the beginning, middle and end of each experience must be linked together in time.[16] There are nuances to each person's way of healing, but the first step is to engage with the experience, to feel and know its impact.

Let me give a fairly simple instance. Josh, a nineteen-year-old college student, came to therapy because he had been in an automobile accident. Since the crash, three weeks previous, he could not concentrate at school, was sleeping badly and his parents sensed that he was "strange and ungrounded." He told me about the accident: he had been driving late at night, had not noticed the other car and had driven straight into it. No one needed medical attention.

We used EMDR, an innovative technique that uses rhythmic eye movements, sound or sensation to help resolve trauma.[17] In our first session, he could reconstruct only some of the accident. He remembered seeing the car too late, the sound of the crash, the air bag exploding and then sitting at the side of the road. In the next session, some of his lightening fast thoughts came back to him. Immediately following the crunch of metal, he was struck by the realization that someone might have been killed. He stopped the car and ran over to the other vehicle to find the occupants shaken but relatively unhurt. He re-experienced his tears of relief.

The third and last session put the whole experience back together in its detail. The thought, "Someone might have been killed" evoked simultaneously a picture of his best friend who had been run over by a drunk driver four years previously. Gory images rose up in his mind causing overwhelming panic. After the accident, he had waited at the side of the road until his mother arrived. In the session his whole body trembled as he recalled his mother holding him.

Following that session, his symptoms resolved. With the reconnection of the traumatizing thoughts, feelings and memories, his vitality reasserted itself. In essence, the frayed ends of his damaged life process had been reunited.

Trauma resolution is not all that it takes to transform vulnerabilities and maintain resilience. There is much more that each of us can do. Care for our physical well-being is essential. It is hard to maintain psychological health in an unhealthy body. Similarly, our intimate relationships need constant attention and support. This is care for the heart. The more we love and care for others, the more we love and care for ourselves, the stronger is our connection with life. It is fear, avoidance and apathy that keep us vulnerable and small.

Life is an opportunity to learn about ourselves and our relationship with the universe. If we back down, it is easy to become overwhelmed. At the same time, we cannot force ourselves to be different. There is an ebb and flow to our own temperament and process that must be acknowledged. A balance of self-discipline and self-care is required. We must respect our natures yet strive to become more. In short, do not coerce yourself yet do not hold back from life.

This is what Arnold Mindell calls working at our "edge."[18] The edge is the limit of our taken-for-granted sense of self, the place where we begin to feel "edgy" and uncomfortable. The place we would sooner avoid than go forward. Part of our mind believes that if we get too close to some scary experience, we will 'go over the edge' and lose ourselves. This is true in a positive as well as negative sense. When we come up against a challenging obstacle, it is an opportunity to extend who we are.

If you find yourself saying or thinking, "I am no good at those kinds of things. I have always been like this. I can't do it." you are at one of your edges. This is a place for self-examination and decision. Instead of accepting your limitation, begin to question deeply what it is you are afraid of. Dig in and find out where and when this feeling started, and whether it is still true.

Most of our edges were installed earlier in life, when they were necessary to protect us from harm. As we grow stronger, we often fail to update our sense of the possible. Examining the way we typically respond to life, we can decide whether it is the right time to do something different. Then we are faced with the dilemma of moving forward or staying still. Sometimes it is appropriate to have patience until we have learned some skill, something has changed spontaneously or the situation becomes right. Then we act, face the new with openness and courage. We extend our resilience beyond the edge.

Vulnerability Transformed

Vulnerabilities are resilience. When transformed, they are exactly what we need for our life journey. Like a rock blocking a river, vulnerability deforms the flow of life yet, if we can just help it shift, it becomes part of the riverbank, resisting erosion. Traumas and hassles, stresses and losses, each create opportunity for further development and expansion. Sometimes, we need outside help to resolve a particular insult to our being. Those are the therapists, physicians and healers whose help can ease the birth of a new way of experiencing. Mostly we have the sole responsibility to face the challenges that life brings.

Each of us has a path to tread. We have our own particular pitfalls and seductions. These are the ways we get lost and misled. For the more damaged, there seems little chance of healing. Viewed with a cynical eye, we judge some people as never learning, never able to change for the better. I have a neighbor who, in my uncharitable moments, falls easily into that category.

But that judgement is not ours to make. We can never fully evaluate a person's life progress or possibility. One step is a mighty accomplishment for someone paralyzed. A single smile may be all that is possible for a man morassed in hatred. Violent criminals *can* become angels of mercy. Every life has more than enough space for forgiveness and transformation.

I remember Jean, the accomplished "Queen of Denial." Cancer riddled her body, scrunching her into a little elf. Yet she remained cheerful and blithe. Death was not an option, she had too many children. Finally, years after her terminal diagnosis, the cancer got a stranglehold, . In those last few days of life something softened and opened. After clinging to life with every grain of her being, after ignoring and avoiding any mention of cancer or dying, she was finally able to let go. Who can know the quality of her experience as she died? That was her own intimate secret.

The Greater process takes us far beyond the limitation of our little self. Seldom can we grasp the immensity and power of that force in our lives. We are too engrossed, looking downward on the ground of our daily lives to take time to raise our eyes to the mountaintops.[19] Sometimes it takes an immense crisis or impending death to have us face the true nature of being alive. The opportunity is always there, in even the simplest experience, if we but recognize it.

Transpersonal Resilience

Physical and psychological resilience can protect us from everyday hassles and crises, but it does not help much with the nature of life itself. The most substantial resilience is based on a sense of the meaningfulness of life. Victor Frankl tells us of those who survived the brutality of Nazi extermination camps. To live through such extremity required a tenacious and profound sense of meaning.[20] Without meaning life becomes pointless and suffering irrelevant. Despair lurks around every corner.

We create meanings. For some it is home and family, for others it is achievement and work. However, to rely only on our experience of outer or inner reality is hazardous. We are changeable beings in a transient world. To have a solid foundation for our being we must connect with the transpersonal, with a meaning big enough to contain all and every experience.

Profound resilience is grounded in the spiritual. Our ultimate models of those who overcome impossible resistance and difficulties to achieve their life tasks are, without exception, profoundly spiritual. Moses, Jesus, Buddha, Mohammed are the pinnacles, the paragons of what is possible. Mahatma Gandhi's non-violent spirituality has been arguably the most potent political force of the last century. Their lives are the stuff of myth and miracle. Yet they are not so different from you and I.

Each day we can read of ordinary people who rise to the extraordinary through faith and inner strength. In my experience, it is those clients who aspire toward wholeness who become exceptional. For some it is through a formal spiritual practice. For others it is more individual and unstructured. Mostly it entails a profound and disciplined commitment to a way of living that invites the presence of the sacred. The arms of this presence hold us in times of complete desperation, a reliable bedrock of resilience that cannot be shaken.

I witnessed this power in Winifred Rushford. One morning she awoke blind with both retinas detached. At the age of 97, there was nothing anyone could do. Taking tea with her soon after, she leaned across the table and confided, "You know, what surprises me most is that it doesn't seem to bother me." She wrote in her autobiography, "Nowadays, increasing blindness makes reading and writing impossible but gives me much leisure in which to meditate."[21]

She was scheduled to run a dream group and see clients the day she died about a year later. Her life had been one of many losses and of long service to others. She spent her early years as a physician in India helping with suffering and squalor. Later in life, she became one of the first women to do training in psychoanalysis.

Fifty years later she was still helping others, showing by example what it is to be in tune with the Greater process. At the end of her life she wrote:

> During this last year there have also been times when it seemed that my own life on earth was ending, and on one particular occasion I recognized that I was very close to death. In the quietness of that occasion there was no fear of what lay beyond; I envisaged the opening of a gate out into a more whole order of being which brought nothing but peace.[22]

This is surrender to a power greater than the personal. This is transpersonal resilience.

CHAPTER 7

Suffering

*Hell goes round and round. In shape it is circular and by
nature it is interminable, repetitive and very nearly
unbearable.*
—Flann O'Brien (from *The Third Policeman*)

*And a woman spoke, saying Tell us of Pain.
And he said:
Your pain is the breaking of the shell that encloses your
understanding.*
—Kahlil Gibran (from *The Prophet*)

Mardy was dark, overweight and scarred. After years of
therapy she was ready to delve deeper into her past. Maybe
confronting the details of her sexual and ritual abuse would help
reconnect all those parts of her fractured personality. She could
hardly get through a day without dissociating. Her dreams were
twisted horrors that woke her sweating in the night.

For three years we struggled with her demons and dredged up
unthinkable and disgusting 'memories.'[1] Her wrists still hurt from
being tied up thirty years earlier. She could still feel the dizziness
and confusion from the drugs, taste the repulsive things thrust into
her mouth.

I almost lost my bearings as the gale force wind of her suffering threatened to sweep me off my feet. Fascinated and sickened, I dreamed of her experiences before she told me, knew what it was like to be 'multiple.' Her indomitable spirit kept pushing us onward and I learned to keep up. Gradually, as the deep infection in her psychic wounds was purged, she began to reconnect with the split off parts of herself. Her healing healed my doubts: human beings can become whole even in the face of overwhelming suffering.

Mardy's experience is extreme. For the most part our suffering is more mundane. We have losses, miseries, and insecurities—ordinary dis-eases of body and soul that drag us down. We become confused in the face of daily trials that drain our resilience and inner strength. Sometimes we move through darker periods toward an increased wholeness and contentment. Other times we seem to slide inexorably into more misery and disturbance.

What makes the difference? Why are we sometimes mobilized by pain and other times mired in suffering? Pain itself is a loud nonspecific signal that tells us something is wrong somewhere in our being. Whether we respond proactively or helplessly depends on a fundamental perception: do we believe that the painful experience does something.

You have a splinter lodged in your flesh, inflamed and festering. Every time you brush against that place, there is a spike of agony. Compare that with the more acute pain of that same splinter as it is removed. Each is excruciating, but the pain of a stuck splinter leads to a cycle of suffering that goes nowhere, except to more suffering. The pain of removal is different—it is purposeful, time limited and easier to bear. It is the pain of healing.

Isabel Duffy, a warm and wise Jungian therapist, puts the distinction succinctly.[2] There are two kinds of suffering: meaningful and meaningless, useful and useless. *Meaningful suffering* has purpose and direction; it moves us toward some future way of being that is more complete. *Meaningless suffering* grinds us down; it is circular, pointless and severs us from communion with the universe and ourselves.

We have to learn to recognize the difference. Often what seems useless and senseless has later benefits of which we are unaware. At other times, to accept and suffer is misguided and even dangerous; to not treat an illness when something can be done is foolhardy. Wisdom is recognizing that difference between useless and useful suffering. This is the heart of "The Serenity Prayer" of Alcoholics Anonymous.[3]

My first big life lesson in suffering happened as an adolescent. I was sixteen, living in a tiny, leaky trailer on a derelict site in Dungarvan, Ireland, alone with my mother. She was drinking and smoking heavily. Constantly unwell, her belly was distending from the pressure of an undiagnosed cancerous tumor. We had little money. I would collect the weekly 'dole' and wander the muddy strand at low tide picking winkles—small, black, snail-like whelks that were sold to consumers in France. Alienated from the rest of the family and avoiding the townspeople, I felt isolated and embarrassed. The worst of it was that I could not imagine it ever ending.

I wrote a note to myself from the depth of misery: "Death would be welcome" and tucked the morbid message away, to be opened at a later date. Not wanting to actively kill myself, I wondered if I would still agree with that statement in some unimagined future. I never found the note again; an unexpected shift of events whirled me away.

Looking back at my adolescent turmoil, I see that at the heart of my suffering were disunities that kept me distant from myself. I was trapped in an inexorable cycle of depressive thoughts and feelings, sundered from myself and those I loved. An understanding listener could have helped release me from most of the useless distress. Yet some part of the suffering was absolutely necessary. It became a teacher for my future profession.

Seeking Wholeness

A psychiatrist would have diagnosed me as suffering from an *Adjustment Disorder with Depressed Mood* or some such categorization.[4] That label belittles my experience. It says nothing of the inexorable inner pressure that ground me down each day or my undirected anger and tortured humiliation at being seen hauling water by the girls in the neighboring convent. It ignores my own attempts to understand myself, the constant questioning about God and how to make sense of being alive. What is worse, it strips my suffering of meaning.

From the perspective of the medical establishment, suffering is bad. Physicians assume that difficult experiences are 'diseases' to be controlled, that some noxious entity has invaded the psyche and needs to be expelled or destroyed. This ignores the basic fact that human beings, like all living things, are *designed* to heal and grow and that discomfort often accompanies that healing. Our ability to self-heal has to be nurtured and supported, not commandeered. When self-healing does not happen, when the suffering cycles endlessly, then we know something is wrong. Suffering itself is not the problem. The problem is the uselessness of that suffering, the fact that it goes nowhere and does nothing.

Human beings can tolerate amazing amounts of affliction. The "Book of Job" is a perfect illustration. But even the smallest discomfort quickly becomes intolerable if it keeps repeating. "Hell goes round and round"—so agree both Flann O'Brien, a writer of bizarre Irish stories, and Dante Alighieri, author of the medieval classic, "The Divine Comedy." Dante's pilgrim visits the nine circles of Hell's *Inferno*. In each the souls are isolated, subjected to the same torture in the same way, without respite for eternity. Each torture exactly fits the nature of their sin.[5]

In traditional Catholic belief, Hellish torment is not simply pain, it arises also from two soul-wrenching realizations. First, the damned know they are separated from God, and second, they know that their suffering and separation will be everlasting. Our own personal Hell has just those qualities: alienation from that which is whole in us and a seemingly endless paralysis. These aspects of useless suffering are what I call *disconnection* and *stuckness*.

In psychotherapy, when clients asks me, "How can I ever feel better?" they are asking me to help them with their suffering—to help them distinguish difficult experiences that have purpose and meaning from those which are useless and obstructing. Often we have to revisit past anguish. The work is not only to heal pain but to discover its meaningfulness.[6] I ask myself, "What is the possible positive intent and consequence of these experiences? In the context of a whole life what could this suffering be for?" If there is no purpose, no direction, then the suffering is meaningless, something has become disconnected, and stuck in that disconnection.

Disconnection

We are born umbilically connected to our mothers. As that physical cord is cut, a psychic connection is already in place. There is no rift for the newborn between self, world and mother. Infants are replete with the Life Force, knowing how to love and be loved, reaching out to be touched and held. In a perfect world, each of us would be encouraged to explore our innate curiosity, vitality and natural wisdom, inspired to connect ever more fully with ourselves and everything. We would grow through each new contact and each new experience. Unfortunately, life is not so simple.

The forces for disconnection are powerful and ever present. Ancestral inheritance, family disturbance, natural and unnatural disasters and even the demands of living create and reinforce our vulnerabilities. Every vulnerability is a different kind of disconnection estranging us from our ability to heal, from our inner nature and from communion with the Greater process. Without realizing, we become a collection of parts separated from the wholeness we crave.

Look at your own or others' children. Already by the age of three a little girl holds her body just like her mother and will unconsciously mimic family mannerisms and speech patterns.[7] Children adopt the attitudes of parents and siblings long before they know their meaning. Violence, racism, sexism and intolerance are learned in the bosom of the family and through endless hours in front of the TV. Many four-year-olds already echo unthinking beliefs; "Bad guys should be locked up and killed. Girls are stupid. I hate Black people." Before we arrive at kindergarten, the schisms of family and society are mirrored in our souls.

Children not only imitate but also internalize the disunities of their parents. The screaming fights, the heavy tension between Mom and Dad are replayed in our inner world. If you listen carefully you may still hear and feel them battling. Parents tell you how to manipulate yourself, how to fit in: "Don't cry, don't get mad, don't make a fuss, pay attention, sit still, follow the rules, work harder." Constant messages direct us to discard part of our needs, wishes, feelings and vitality. Before long we do not need the outer voice as there is a tyrant inside directing our every action.

School and work further reinforce the fractures demanding that we relegate parts of who we are to the basement of our being. Do you remember sitting in a boring classroom listening to an equally boring teacher? Naturally, when nothing stimulating is going on, your attention slips into the world of fantasies. You look out the window, imagining being out in the sunshine. Suddenly you are jerked back to the classroom, "Hey you! Pay attention and stop daydreaming!" The teacher is shouting at you and all eyes turn your way. A breeze of giggles wafts through the room and you flush with embarrassment. This is no place to let down your guard. Learn quickly if you want to avoid further humiliation—it is not safe to imagine.

Imposed and learned disconnections become rooted deep in

our adult personality. Every society decides which experiences and behaviors are relevant, necessary and valued. We figure out those parts of our selves that are acceptable to family and culture. The rest have to go. Before long, we are unable to notice what has gone missing. Like a pruned tree, the lopped limbs whither and die.

Divorce of the Body

Human nature is amazingly malleable. Unlike other organisms, very little of what we feel, think and do is innately programmed—we can choose. Yet we are easily trapped by the unconscious assumptions of inherited belief systems that are more oppressive than any instinct. In this culture, for three hundred and fifty years, the human mind and human body have been conceptually split, disconnected. So deeply ingrained is this Cartesian divide that we hardly notice, yet it permeates all our experience.[8] For all the fact that we have conquered certain diseases and extended life, we suffer from a deeper sickness, we are estranged from our own physical nature.

In modern life the body is a thing, an 'It', to be managed and controlled. [9] Media portray only the perfect, the attractive and the young. Many struggle to make their bodies live up to unrealistic expectations of remaining beautiful, fit, healthy and undemanding. Dieting and exercise become compulsive, even life-threatening. We fill our bodies with unneeded food and chemicals, and then feel betrayed when they mutiny. So we take it to a physician to be fixed, ignoring what it is trying to tell us about our lives. The worst 'betrayals', of course, are aging, sickness and death. The modern maxim seems to be "Bodies are meant to take abuse and stay young and beautiful eternally."

I have noticed patterns of connection between illness and blocked process. These are not the simplistic explanations found in popular books: asthma means repressed anger; ulcers are caused by stress; cancer means something is eating at you. Human beings are too complex and unique for simple explanations of any disease.

When something interferes with our healing ability, there is both an individual and a general pattern of disconnection involved.

Certain neurological and autoimmune disorders seem to attack people who drive themselves beyond their natural capacity. The fierceness of this drivenness turns fight/flight hormones full on, undermining the integrity of the immune system. The natural need for calm relaxation is ignored and eventually the nervous system collapses. These individuals are often not fully embodied. They live just a little forward of their physical selves as if dragging it along like a heavy sack. The subtle warning signals of disunion between body and psyche are ignored until they reach a point of no return.

Still the outcome is far from predictable. I have seen one woman die of multiple sclerosis within two years of her diagnosis and another recover completely in the same time period. A terminal diagnosis of cancer may spell death for one and renewed life for another. What makes the difference? Working with different people, I often sense who has the possibility to heal their illness against all odds. I think of it as the ability to fully accept and look the illness in the face while at the same time not giving in—no denial and no self pity. The individual must be willing to become whole, to connect fully with the deeper process and its healing ability.

Trauma and prolonged distress disrupts that connection. The majority of clients with severe psychological difficulties also have physical ailments. Gynecological problems and fibromyalgia are prevalent in women who have been sexually abused. Abuse leaves a scar, not only in the psyche but also on the way the body is connected to the energetic process of the whole person. When vitality is withdrawn from some part of our corporeal self, that part begins to wither and die.

Working with a young woman in trance who had chronic painful fibromyalgia around her shoulder, a spontaneous memory came. Her father's prelude to the molestation was to gently stroke her back. Without moving a muscle she tried to get away from his hand and its sickening touch. Like a dried raisin she shriveled up inside, smaller and smaller, desperate to erase her body's sensations. As she put it, "I had to get out of that part of my body."

In the worst cases there is damage, not only to the ability to heal but also the will to live. Life-threatening diseases are often found in those whose 'survival instinct' has been compromised through overwhelming life events. Natural healing and the urge to stay alive can be broken. When I work with someone with severe illness, the first thing to discover is if the will to live is intact. If that has been disconnected, the essential spark of life will fade away.

The first time I saw Gary he was completely distraught. Over the years, he had noticed and ignored the growing numbness and weakness in his hands and arms until it became nearly impossible to pick up a cup of coffee. When Gary had gone back after his check up, the doctor seemed really pleased with himself—he had diagnosed a rare, deteriorating neurological disorder that causes death by choking.

Gary was devastated. He now believed the future held only paralysis and a horrible end. Almost immediately his condition started getting worse. His body was doing what the doctor told it to do. He toyed with killing himself but it was not an option. Earlier in his life, comatose from a serious suicide attempt, he had experienced the living hell of the self-murderer. He felt blessed to have been given a second chance.

We worked together on his depression and hopelessness. Years later, Gary is still living an independent life. He has lost some abilities, but always his ingenuity has found a way through. More important, he no longer sees death as a monster looming just around the corner. He knows that his body will do the best it can to keep alive. If not for his spiritual experiences, Gary would have killed himself. Without help to rid himself of the toxic suggestions of the doctor, he may have given up.

Physical illness is not all psychological, but at the deepest level there is no separation between mind and body. Every experience is a neurological pattern, a physical event. Every choice we make resonates throughout our whole being, material and immaterial. Physical processes are part of who we are and our body requires that we remember. If we treat our body as a disconnected *thing*, we are courting illness and suffering. To be a human in this world is to be embodied, to be fully connected to ourselves and our lives.

Disconnections of the Self

Matthew was very depressed when he first came to see me. Tall and thin, with a permanent lean, like a tree caught in a high wind, he told a story of misery and emptiness. The high forehead and sad bespectacled eyes hid a penetrating, critical mind that never stopped. He hated his job entering data into a computer in a tiny cubicle. He hated going home to his silent apartment. He took a sort of twisted amusement in mentally devising different ways to kill himself. Thankfully none were satisfactory to his critical mind.

Early on in therapy he told me a dream: *A man dressed in battle fatigues jumps to catch a rope swinging over a pool of water. He misses, falls and breaks his neck. Lying helpless, the back of his body is darkly immersed in the muddy water, the front of his body still clean.*

The dream tells us of Matthew's brokenness. His conscious self is split from the rest of his being. There is a chasm between the darker hidden side and his bright critical mind. The battle for his life is almost lost—he cannot stop himself from falling. The disconnections between head and body, above and below paralyses him and keeps him immobile.

Western culture is not comfortable with the messiness of bodily functions and the non-rationality of the deeper process living in the body. Dreams, intuitions and unconscious ways of

152

knowing are downgraded or relegated to the weird world of artists, psychics and psychoanalysts. Everyone dreams, but how often do we pay attention to these deeper urgings? At every moment our unconscious is working away, just below awareness, keeping everything going. Yet we seldom remember, seldom extend a feeling of gratitude or acceptance toward that essential part of ourselves. We keep it secret and separate—disconnected. No wonder it sometimes rebels.

Matthew was not only divided from his natural self, he also suffered from that most common male disconnection—the split between feeling heart and thinking mind. Boys learn early not to be 'wimps', not to cry or express the softer emotions. These are discounted and ignored. In the West only the 'strong' and dominating expression of anger is OK, it is powerful and 'manly.'

For women, on the other hand, it is power and purpose that often becomes suppressed, leaving a feeling of emptiness and inadequacy. Many creative women are entrapped by their unconscious assumptions, never realizing their own strength and courage.

Every inner disconnection manifests in outer experience.[10] When a man is out of touch with his feelings, he will be unable to enter into intimate and satisfying relationships. If a woman cannot find her power, how can she be effective and influential in the world? Connection with the world and those around us reflects our connection with ourself. The ability to be joined, intimate and engaged requires a whole being. If we are estranged from ourselves how can we relate to others?

When we are not internally harmonious, not aware of ourselves as whole beings, our experience of the Greater process is elusive. Regardless of a professed belief in God, regardless of attendance at places of worship, regardless of whether we think we know spirituality, without direct contact, the Greater process is a myth, a phantasm. *Spirituality is immediate experience of something greater, profound and beyond our ideas and expectations.* The Greater process provides meaning and purpose to our existence. To be disconnected from that universal power is to be lost.

By adulthood, for many, the springs of childhood exuberance have seeped away. 'Realistic' cynicism takes it place and life becomes a wasteland. If you take stock, can you truly say that you are *in* your own life deeply enough? What parts of your being are discordant, unsettling you with a furtive sense of disquietude?

Minor ailments, compulsive behaviors and troublesome relationships are familiar, ordinary and unquestioned, they form the unnoticed background of our everyday life. Do we listen to these messages telling us that something is amiss?

Only when suffering becomes bad enough do we seek help. The internal voice that tells us to persevere, to be strong and self-reliant often serves us well. It is misguided when we are broken. We must face the reality of our own incompleteness before we can begin to heal.

Disconnected Relationship

A common scenario: I get into a fight with my life partner. It all started when I came through the door after a horrible day at work and she was less than sympathetic—actually abrupt and dismissive of my exhaustion. She didn't even notice my sighs and heavy footsteps. I try to listen to her catalog of hassles with the children and shopping but the house and everything is a mess. We start sniping at each other about inconsequentials, though the underlying theme is, "I had a harder day than you and I need attention." Soon the kids are fighting and upset and we all sit in a heavy silence at the dinner table. This can't be good for digestion but how are we to undo it all without looking foolish or vulnerable? I'm not going to be the first to say I'm sorry.

What happened? I brought my disconnection home. Then at that most sensitive time as we meet again after a separation, our partnership failed to reunite. Soon that disconnection spread through the family, spilling over into the children and the whole evening. Old hurts were reactivated, reinforcing the resistance to reconciliation. Unwilling to open to each other we could easily remain stuck in separate camps, the rift never closing. Eventually the family would disintegrate. From such small beginnings are divorces made.[11]

Without awareness and compassion, we inflict our disconnections on those around us. My unhealed wounds are not an issue if they do not affect anyone else, but that's impossible. I *am* my family, community, society and the wider world. My disturbance is disturbance for all. Internal splits and deadening are not simply the causes of our personal misery. As they adulterate wider and wider relationships, those splits become tendrils of evil.

When I hear that as a child, Dawn was locked in a dog pen with a snarling German Shepherd as a babysitter and randomly beaten, I cannot be convinced that "all is well in the best of all possible worlds." The damage inflicted by a mother's uncontrolled rages is not useful or meaningful to a child. Dawn's mother obviously had her own pain from the unhealed chasms in her being. Her 'sin' is her unwillingness to recognize, own and bear it. She heaped her torment onto her daughter. To give another your own suffering is to compound the pain. To create more pain, more disconnections in the universe is to create un-life, to create evil.

Corruption is caused by things out of place, by disconnections and constrictions in the Life Force. If something is not in its right place, if it has become separated from the benign constraints of the whole, then it is in danger of becoming toxic. If the discomfort and hurt we inflict on others has no positive meaning, does not lead to some greater good, then it is wrong.

The extreme example of disconnected relationship is the 'sociopathic personality,' a person who has no sense of community with other human beings. He does not belong, does not feel empathy. Without social and emotional connection all behaviors are possible. What does he care for others' pain? All that matters is whether they are of use or not. Sociopathic behavior spreads disturbance, so inevitably, society responds with harsh punitive measures, further disconnecting that individual—and so the cycle continues.

We all have sociopathic tendencies. We try to get our own way at the expense of others. When another driver cuts you off or takes 'your' parking space it is easy to make them bad and inhuman in your mind. Then you turn on your righteous indignation and feel superior. You are lifted up and they are degraded in your eyes. But you have fallen into the sin of disconnection. Whenever we turn another person, another race, another nation into something less than human in our minds, we tear the fabric of humanity. Martin Buber, the great Jewish philosopher calls this the "I-It" relationship, the root of all manipulation and abuse.

It is impossible to harm what we are part of or what is a part of us. When I was an adolescent I burnt a design into the skin of my forearm. I remember vividly, not the pain but the extreme resistance of my body to harming itself. It rebelled with all its strength. I cannot do you harm if we are both part of the same whole—part of the body of humanity.

Disconnection creates disturbance throughout our being and our lives, and from there into the lives of others. How we are with our loved ones, and even more so with those we do not really care for, is a reflection of how we feel about ourselves. When our feelings are blocked, our hearts hardened, relationships decay, conflict erupts around us and there is no harmony. Conflict breeds conflict, disconnection creates more disunity spreading in ever widening ripples over the face of our world.

I have a friend who translated speeches from Russian to English at the nuclear disarmament talks during the 1970's. He would return from those talks despairing. He could see no common ground, no basis of trust or cooperation. His job was to scrutinize the other side's translation for any mistake, just as they watched him for every incorrect nuance of meaning. Everything was suspect, nuclear war was just an unthinking insult away.

Have you been in a meeting in which there is no commonality? Each person has his own agenda with no compromise, disagreements and arguments become more and more heated and entrenched. These meetings do not produce anything creative and usually end in disorder as the disturbance becomes intolerable. This is what happens with all systemic disturbance. This is what is happening in our culture.

Only a society divorced from itself and the natural world can rape the earth of its bountiful resources. Only when a country decides that the 'enemy' is less human, more evil and deserving of punishment can it send its planes, missiles and armies to butcher men, women and children. Every war requires propaganda to create alienation from, and hatred for, the other side. Otherwise a feeling, thinking human being, just like me or you is who we destroy.

We blame others for the suffering we impose. We delude ourselves that this suffering is for a purpose. It is necessary. Yet it is easy to tell if that is true. All we have to ask ourselves is, "Am I acting from a place of alienation and fear—or caring and compassion?" If we are disconnected from that person or people, if we are entrenched and invested in that disconnection, we are choosing to spread useless suffering into the world.

Gandhi expressed this point so beautifully, "Experience convinces me that permanent good can never be the outcome of untruth and violence."[12] Only actions that are engendered by love, by a sense of connection and belonging, can be healing.

Stuckness

Cycles of connecting and disconnecting are part of the natural flow of life. When we sleep, we are disconnected for a period from our own consciousness. Sometimes we want to be with people, sometimes we need solitude. Relationship becomes impossibly tedious if we *have* to be with the same person every moment of every day. Even a usually loving contact can feel oppressive if it never changes. There is a flowing rhythm to healthy relationship.

These natural cycles feel different from disconnections imposed on us. Unexpected injury threatens our coherence. If we suddenly get sick, break a bone, someone dies or our relationship becomes a minefield of conflict, we suffer pain. More often than not, we find the strength to physically heal, to forgive and let go of hurt and resentment, to grieve and say goodbye to those who are gone. The disconnection mends and we are whole again.

Our human system is remarkably resilient. It constantly finds ways to heal and reconnect.[13] When it cannot, something is wrong. The difference between a disconnection that is a passing phase and one that causes meaningless suffering is the quality of *stuckness*.[14]

What do I mean by stuckness? Let me give a common example of normal psychological healing and how it gets obstructed.

Someone you love dies. You feel disoriented, wake in the night thinking about him, and find yourself tired and despondent most days. It is worse two to three weeks after the death when the funeral and fuss dies down. Now there is the emptiness to face. You regret not having been there at the death, wish that you could have said certain unspoken words. You sense a subtle irrational irritation with him for dying just then, in that way. Mostly it is just sad.

After a few months, you wake some days feeling out of sorts but do not consciously associate it with the death. The anniversary of the death, however, hits you hard. The grief gets easier with time in a rhythmic wave of misery that decreases in depth and power the further it travels from the loss. After a couple of years, you often visit your memories of that person with a poignant sadness that is rich and easy. Your natural bereavement has healed the disconnections.

But what if it gets stuck? Then the sadness and anger transform into a debilitating grayness that never shifts. Thoughts of the loved-one become endless ruminations that recycle with no relief. In the worst situations, a kind of frozen shrine to the dead becomes entombed in the self. Desperate clinging to photographs and belongings mark that shrine.

I have seen a bedroom of a dead child in perfect order, awaiting his return from school after six years. He died suddenly in a traffic accident but his mother refused to let him go. Her life is still on hold and will stay so until she dies. Her inability to allow reality to be as it is keeps her insolubly stuck in grief.

Disconnected stuckness is like a cancer. Cancer cells duplicate without limit, without regard for the whole body, their growth mechanism stuck full on. It is as if those cells do not listen, do not respond to messages from the rest of the body. They just keep growing. Useless suffering is similar, it just keeps growing, doing nothing for our being.

In contrast, when we catch a cold or flu our immune system creates a range of uncomfortable symptoms—fevers, runny nose, aches and pains. As uncomfortable as these may be, the suffering does something. It is fundamental to the healing.

Fear and Healing

How do experiences heal? As children, we rely on our relationship with caregivers to support inner healing. We run to a loving parent for comfort and care when we are hurt or afraid and the experience mends naturally. As we get older, aspects of these early relationships are internalized as templates of healing. An inner environment is created that allows disturbance to resolve naturally. But just as the outer environment was imperfect and often unsupportive, the inner environment reflects that imperfection. Limiting beliefs, self-doubt, insecurities and dependence on the outer world undermines our resilience.

In its most universal aspect, we cannot connect with inner healing because we have become *retracted in fear*—fear that is not anxiety but a deeper sense of terror or angst, a quality of clinging on for dear life. It is that clinging, what the Buddhists call *tanha*, that fuels repetitive vicious cycles. The Buddha, in the *Four Noble Truths* tells us that the origin of suffering is compulsive attachment. When tanha ceases, suffering ceases. Fear of the unknown, the uncontrollable, impels clinging.

Let me give an all too common example. Alice has everything she needs materially—beautiful home, plenty of money, help around the house. Her life is the image of the 'American Dream.' Beneath the facade she is miserable, trapped in a maze of depressed agitation. Small hassles and trials spiral her emotions out of control. Childless, because "that is what they agreed", her life has no shape, no point. Yet she will not face even the possibility of separation from her distant and critical husband who pays for it all.

Alice remembers the optimism and excitement of college days, studying literature and writing, but those days are long gone. Now she never puts pen to paper—too busy, too stressed. She wants me to take away the anxiety, to make it feel better. But there is nothing to put in its place, only emptiness. All attempts at change are thwarted by her fear.

The demands that life and her deeper self make are too much for Alice. She needs to stay stuck to be safe. Part of her knows it is a false security but she continues to block her ears to the quiet voice inside that says "live", even as it gets louder and more insistent. Already the conflict expresses itself through anxiety and panic. What if it speaks in the physical language of breast cancer or heart palpitations? Maybe her only hope is for some crisis to stimulate her inner strength and get her moving again.

In clinging to the known, Alice manipulates her inner and outer reality to be what she wishes it would be, rather than what it is.[15] She wants her life to be different without it ever changing.

She wants to feel better without looking at what causes her suffering. Her clinging creates more disconnection and more stuckness in an expanding spiral.

Stuckness is a whirlpool in the flow of a river. Once formed, anything caught in that swirling eddy cycles endlessly. All gets drawn in to support and perpetuate the stuckness. The influence of the vortex extends ever outward, affecting more and more aspects of our being.

Stuckness in the Psyche

Alice suffered from depression and anxiety, both common examples of disconnected stuckness. To put it simply, chronic anxiety is stuck fear; depression is stuck sadness or anger. When fear and sadness do not shift and change with circumstance something is wrong.

I remember the harrowing distress I felt in my adolescence. Functioning and looking fine on the outside, I was tortured internally. The distress of depression is more than a passing mood or state. Clouds of misery hang around interminably, like a severe bout of flu. All inner reserves are depleted, the depression draining vitality and awareness.

So it is with chronic anxiety. Every situation is experienced as an imminent disaster. The person is harrowed by doubts and insecurities, not knowing how to relax and go with the flow. The fight-flight endocrine response is stuck full on. The connection to human curiosity and courage goes missing.

Most acute depressions and fears are responses to difficult life events. Fred cannot concentrate at work or sleep at night since his wife left him. Jane struggles to return to work after years of child rearing and is tortured by self-doubt and feelings of inadequacy. Their distress is, in some sense, a natural response to the struggles of life and their own vulnerabilities. It reflects the stuckness of something in their lives.

Anxiety and depression are the obvious faces of stuckness. *But any aspect of our being that has a compulsive quality, that does not exhibit flexibility and creativity, is suspect.* Less obvious pathology disguises itself as culturally valued attributes such as competitiveness, drive, ambition and even nurturing. The successful businessman, who takes his phone and fax to the pool when on holiday is stuck without knowing it. The son who sends his dirty laundry home from college and the mother who washes it are both stuck. Affliction hides where we least notice.

Whenever we are unable to spontaneously think a thought, feel a feeling or complete an action, something is stuck. Whenever we continue to think or feel or act when it is no longer necessary, something is stuck. When we are unable to be present, aware and respond with compassion, something is stuck. When we are lost to ourselves, overwhelmed by impulses and experiences that are uninvited, something in our being is stuck and cannot move on. If we always respond to our relationships in the same way, we are stuck.

Stuckness in thinking is prejudice, the inability to shift perspective or see the other person's point of view. Stuck feelings are those emotions that do not resolve, fears that refuse to change, sadness that becomes depressive, smoldering rage that never calms down. Stuck behaviors are actions that are repetitive, sterile and indifferent to the needs of the moment. All these are our habitual and insensitive reactions to everyday life. We recognize them as lifeless and dull, or recurringly maladaptive. Suddenly we realize we are stuck in the same old pattern again.

If that catalog is true, it seems that we are all stuck most of the time. Maybe only those who are enlightened or dying are able to avoid the traps of life. The important thing seems to be whether the *stuckness is itself stuck.* I may have a writer's block that lasts for months. I am stuck, yet I know from experience that something will unexpectedly shift and the block will dissolve. So the stuckness is not totally stuck. It is not the same as a repetitive pattern that grips and never lets go.

An agoraphobic fears to leave her home. Maybe something happened in the past—fainting or vomiting in the street—that fueled her apprehension. Now she is frightened of some nameless, catastrophic humiliation, so she avoids leaving home. What locks her behavior into place is a foreboding of the terror of going outside. Not only can she not leave, she cannot *think* of leaving the house. The noose gets tighter—fear of fear, avoidance of avoidance, stuck stuckness.

Many people have phobias, particularly fears of animals such as snakes, spiders and dogs. A dog phobia is one of the simplest examples of stuckness. The sight of a dog, no matter how innocuous, leads to fear and flight. All dogs are treated as identical and the reaction to any particular dog is similar to every other one. The response is always compulsive anxiety and avoidance.

For the phobic, as the dog gets closer, fear escalates, apprehension turns to anxiety, to panic and finally to overwhelming terror. The phobic person flees, bypassing any positive experience that might change the dread; the vicious cycle is closed.

Obsessions and compulsions are particularly virulent forms of stuckness. Ruminating thoughts that go round and round are obsessions. Actions that have an uncontrollable authority over the self are compulsions. Compulsions include all addictions and all problems of impulse control. Substance abuse and sex/relationship addictions are among the commonest problems seen by therapists. But compulsions come in less obvious guise. Habitual avoidance and procrastination, extreme competition and need for control of others, fanaticism, bigotry, explosive anger— are all examples of some form of compulsive process. If you are always late (or early) for appointments you are probably caught in a minor compulsion.

In its most disturbing form, Obsessive-Compulsive Disorder

(OCD), compelling thoughts and actions take over the whole of a person's waking life. Usually there are powerful and inescapable impulses to check or clean. The sufferer washes his or her hands until they are chapped and bleeding, vacuums the house endlessly or checks and rechecks the locked doors at night.

One of my first therapeutic failures was a young man diagnosed with classic OCD. Like the majority of these sufferers, one of his parents was an obsessive cleaner. He had taken on the family pattern and amplified it out of control. He could not go anywhere without simultaneously looking up and down trying to dodge birds that might poop on him and sidestepping any dog excrement.

His fears of pollution were so extreme that he took two or three baths a day, spent hours on the toilet, washed his hands constantly and walked in the street, off the sidewalk, his head swiveling up, down and around at every step. The compulsion permeated every aspect of his life and personality. I tried everything in my limited repertory with little success. I eventually referred him on to someone more experienced.

Recognizing Our Patterns

How are we to recognize our own obsessions, compulsions and minor phobias? I have a personal maxim that helps me decide personally and in therapy whether a process is really stuck: *If the same thing happens in the same (or very similar) way more than three times in a row, or for more than a month at a time, then it is problematic.* This is a simple reminder to recognize stuckness but not get it confused with the normal ups and downs of life. A few days of sadness and melancholy is not depression. A spike of anxiety before a flight is not a phobia of flying. A fight with your partner does not mean divorce.

It takes courage and dedication to look ourselves in the eye and see our shortcomings clearly. There are layers of protection surrounding our deepest pain and disturbance. I remind clients that therapy, learning about yourself, is often a rough road. The rewards are incomparable, but it doesn't always feel good. Yet this suffering is important, it is worthwhile.

Recurring discomfort is our most useful guide to disconnection. As we look to whatever is most uncomfortable, we are likely to find our next task. I lived in a shared household in my twenties and whenever a new roommate arrived, I found that person intolerably irritating after about three weeks. The experience was so consistent I realized it could not be them, it had to be me. With a shock I saw how blind I was to my own projections and how compelling was the impulse to make them wrong. The irritation hid my unease at connecting intimately, my fear of being swallowed up in community.

What clued me in was that my irritation was cyclical and recurring. Stuckness always creates the same form of experience. So whenever we notice our discomfort, the next thing to notice is whether this has happened before and how often. As the saying goes: *dysfunction is the same damn thing again and again; health is one damn thing after another.* Beware of the same damn thing!

We have to be discriminating. It is not always clear whether something is the same of not. If I always get stressed by driving, always feel miserable on Mondays, always feel distant from my wife after sex, there is clearly a stuck pattern. But what if it only happens sometimes? What if there is another factor that I haven't noticed? Say I only get stressed driving if I travel on a certain highway and I usually avoid that one. What if I only feel miserable on Mondays when I am feeling unappreciated by my manager? Sex is usually tender and loving except when certain things my wife says subtly reminds me of my bossy sister.

Our own avoidance strategies and the complexity of processes hide negative patterns right under our noses. The limitation to our awareness and understanding makes it impossible to see the whole picture. So how can I see the beam in my own eye, rather than the mote in yours? The answer is both outside us and deeper within.

Transforming Suffering

Our very selves are a battleground of competing forces. That is why we suffer. On the one hand, the demands and trials of the world cause schisms in our beings. On the other hand, our deeper process seeks to create greater connectivity and coherence. This is the fertile struggle between un-life and life that bids us keep striving and changing.[16]

In this encounter we all get stuck, we all get lost sometimes. We fall prey to the snares of ego and superficiality and try to stop the movement of life. Then we suffer without purpose. We lose contact with the flow of the Life Force.

So how can we again enter into a healing flow? We know that true healing is not under conscious control. Even the smallest cut cannot be made to mend faster than it naturally heals. When someone dies there is no avoiding the pain of grief. The torments, hassles and disappointments of everyday life cause us anguish. In order to transform ordinary suffering we must face and embrace the pain. Then, as we recognize our failures and inflexibility, we can take steps to reconnect.

Imagine you are upset and angry with a good friend or lover. You had a fight and his attitude seemed cruel and thoughtless. He let you down, betrayed you. Nothing is resolved. Now his words and the words of your unspoken, perfect rejoinder go round and round in your head as you try to sleep. You are stirred up, unsettled and ready to never see him again. What should you do?

First, you have to accept the hurt and bitterness you feel. Your natural impulse is to blame him, and he may be to blame. But if you want this suffering to be useful, to stop recycling, you have to delve deeper into its meaning. What is this pain trying to tell you?

In truth, you are probably clinging to a distorted reality. You are holding some unconscious expectation of how you want him to be. Is that expectation realistic or are you deceiving yourself?

Can you see and accept him as he is, rather than how you wish? If you loosen your attachment to how you think it *should* be, your experience will start to flow naturally again.

Now, you must decide on an appropriate action to reconnect your inner and outer worlds. If it is right for you to part, then be decisive—cut the psychic ties cleanly and unquestionably. If not, you may have to say you are sorry even though you think you did nothing wrong. When we take on the suffering of a whole situation consciously, with open heart, we create more space for connection.

Meaningless suffering is lifeless and repetitive. Yet we cannot make the pain disappear, we cannot command ourselves to be different. Only as we take the suffering on consciously and willingly, embrace it as part of the tasks and texture of life, does it change. Then suffering becomes impregnated with meaning. This is an 'ego sacrifice', a letting go of the wishes and desires of the small self in the service of something greater. Through grace and insight the pain becomes part of us and we move on.

Why is it so hard to let go of useless suffering? It is because we hate to admit we are wrong. We do not want to face our stuckness and brokenness. When confronted with deficiencies, our sense of self feels wounded. We grieve a lost vision of who we thought we were. Then it is so easy to get lost in self-pity or self-loathing, another cycle of purposeless pain.

What is required is ruthless integrity. We must recognize and accept our failings in order to do something about them. This is the acute agony of healing and wholeness. In the face of this pain all we can do is surrender, allow ourselves to let go into and through the transformative suffering. Our bodies, minds and spirits have hidden resources that are almost never fully tapped. We *will* be helped.

To accept, recognize and grieve our disconnected parts invites the Life Force to revitalize our being. Trusting in the movement of life, in the inherent purposefulness of everything, is like opening up to an unknown layer of support. Once we connect with that ever-available underlying Greater process our experience becomes infused with meaning. Through reconnection with ourselves and with the transcendent, suffering transforms beyond expectation.

PART III

The Path Toward Wholeness

CHAPTER 8

Connection and Wholeness

Midway between mortals and the gods, love is a Great
Spirit that connects the earthly and the heavenly.
—Plato, (from *The Symposium*)

The complete human being, the man who has become
whole (and therefore "holy"), is he who unites the
universal with the individual...
—Lama Anagarika Govinda

I was eighteen before I learned to reconnect. My adolescent
turmoil had driven a wedge between me and the world, between
me and myself. The years from sixteen to eighteen had seen an
intense search for some spiritual path, some guidance as to what I
should do with my life. That search culminated in my "opening"
in Subud, a spiritual organization in which people receive a
contact with the Life Force. Even with my hesitations and doubts
a subtle vibration was beginning to move in my inner feelings.

I was living in a hostel for adolescent boys who had come to
Dublin to find work. It was large and impersonal with dormitories
of eight beds, a cavernous eating hall and several smaller
recreation rooms. There were not many rules: pay dues on time, no
drink or drugs, keep your area clean and tidy, get in before the
doors were locked at eleven o'clock.

171

Intellectual and shy, I did not fit with the boisterous, sporty crowd. I remained an alienated outsider. Each evening, after work in a soulless office selling cans and packaging, I would slink off to the Irish National Library. There, in the green baize stillness, I would request obscure mystical books mostly on Buddhism and Gnostic Christianity. They would arrive dusty and unread from somewhere in the bowels of the building and I would try to decipher their esoteric obscurities.

One late night lying in bed, I felt this unusual warm stirring sensation in my chest. Images of my family came unbidden to my mind. My eyes filled with tears of gratitude as I realized how I felt connected to them, though we hardly wrote or communicated. Tender thoughts of friends and even the other boys asleep around me, amplified that feeling.

I realized, with a jolt, that I was experiencing Love. It grew stronger. An immeasurable connection with some compassionate force, I could not call it 'God,' grew so intense it seemed it might burst my chest. For a little while, I was connected lovingly to everyone and everything. The experience echoed through my being for a few days and then subsided, leaving an indelible imprint: *Everything is connected and I am part of that connection.*

Truths are profoundly simple and inexhausively complex. Such a truth is *connection*—that everything emerges only through the joining of parts to form a different and unexpected whole. Connection and reconnection create all the reality we know, our experience, our being, and our universe. Without a gravitational bond, the earth would whirl away from the sun and we would be flung from the earth. The attraction of positive and negative charge unites each spinning atom into a whole. Even at the sub-atomic level there are mysterious connections between particles that cause them to move in a coordinated dance.

Relationship holds it all together, joins all of creation and fashions something greater than we can encompass. Every person, every group, every community is a pattern of related parts connected in some way to all others. You are part of your family, your society and the human race. Simultaneously, you are the product of all your experiences, all the organic processes happening in your body, all the molecules and energies that vibrate ceaselessly. All of these are you, just as you are a part of something more and greater. What holds it all together is connection. What allows you to grow and develop is reconnection.

What exactly do I mean by connection and connectivity? Certainly it is not randomly putting together two or more elements. If your body was taken apart, the limbs, organs, bones, muscles and blood separated out, there would be an organic mess but no living organism. Only when the elements are assembled in a particular configuration, only when they are put together in that one, exact way, does your specific living body emerge. Connection is the glue that binds everything together to create something more than the parts. It is the *spirit of wholeness.*

Every rounded action, every intimate contact with another person, every deeply integrated experience connects us to the Greater process. Spirituality is not outside our ordinary life; it is inherent in the texture of our being, in the bindings that hold us together and connects us to everything. To write a completed poem is a spiritual act; to look your child in the eye with love is a spiritual act; to follow an insight to its utmost conclusion is a spiritual act. More than anything, to become more complete, to become more coherent is our spiritual task. It is not the specifics of what we do, but the realization of a connection inward or outward that makes everything sacred.

Connecting to Our Senses

Everywhere in life is the urge to connect. Who can see a baby animal or infant without wanting to touch it, stroke it? The presence of a newborn tunes our being into our own birthing, our own beginnings. Some part of us knows the freshness and newness of coming into the world, the time when our "doors of perception" were open and clean.[1]

Arriving in Boulder, Colorado from dreary England, I could hardly believe my eyes. The mountains rising rugged and pristine from the edge of the city looked like a painted backdrop from an old Western movie. The detail of rock and tree outlined against the blue sky were so perfect, so vibrant. I had trouble driving, craning my neck around, distracted by the scenery.

Routine and jaded expectation dull our perceptions. I wondered how long it would take before I, like many around me, would take that magnificence for granted, begin not to notice. Now, after ten years, my eyes are no longer innocent. To see and feel the impact of familiar beauty takes attention and effort. I have to wipe away the haze of expectation that films reality, strive to reconnect with the raw image once again. To see, hear, feel, taste and smell fully is to participate in the wonder of creation, it *is* an act of creation.

Our senses are not passive receptors, they are active organs of contact. Eyes that illuminate our inner vision are windows of the soul. We do not simply peer out of these windows, we reach through them to seize whatever attracts us.[2] Touch, taste, smell and sound are our points of contact with the energy of the universe. When you listen intently to a symphony or rock song, when you gaze in awe at a Michelangelo or Cezanne, when you breath deeply the fragrance of a rose, you are connecting more fully.

We *feel* our way into the world, through newborn cheek and suckling mouth against breast, through brush of skin against skin. To know intimately is to touch—run a hand over rough bark, feel the silky softness of a peach skin, rest your hand on a friend's arm. How could we make love without touch? Touch is the essence of contact. Whenever we disconnect, we 'lose touch.'

To be in touch with ourselves, with our sensual experience, is

174

to become more whole. The more we accept our embodied nature the more we enjoy life. We are physical organisms in a material world. If we get too abstract, too distant from our bodies and senses, we lose the texture and satisfactions of outer reality. We lose ourselves.

We experience the world most vividly, vibrantly when we are quiet inside. If our attention is drawn inward by worries, conflicts and insistent concerns, the outer world recedes. For the depressed person, there are no colors, just a gray film encrusting reality. Only as we become more internally connected, more at home with ourselves, can we relate fully to what is outside of us. If we are out of touch with who we are, we will be out of touch with others. The quality of our own being is reflected in the mirror of our relationships.

Connecting to Others

Humans cannot not relate.[3] Relationship is that magical, mysterious force that creates a new combination, a new whole that is "more and different from the sum of the parts."[4] Each time I allow myself to connect, unexpected possibilities emerge. No longer alone in the universe, through relationship I am jolted into a different way of being. A richer, more complex process emerges. The deeper and more intimate the connection, the more fertile the result.

Relationship is a *resonance* of our vibrating process with that of another. When we meet someone for the first time, we unconsciously test the 'tonal' quality of the other person's vibration. Some we can never attune to, their reverberation is too dissonant, too different from ours. We avoid them and they remain strangers.

Others are immediately familiar, we deeply and easily connect with their inner rhythm and intuitively understand their experience. These people become our friends. They have a resonating process that harmonizes easily with our own. When we are with them, a synergy happens that takes us beyond our narrow sense of self.

There is an outdoor walking mall in Boulder where people congregate to shop, eat and watch the street entertainers. I like to look at the people milling around or sitting. I notice two kinds, those who are connected energetically to others and those who are not. The disconnected, who may even be with company, look tense, pensive, encapsulated. They are separate and isolated even amidst the people around them. You can see this isolation most vividly on any crowded subway in a big city. Each person draws into a tight bundle of energy that does not connect with anyone else even when physically touching.

Now watch what happens when contact is made. Maybe the person sees a friend or makes eye contact with a child. Immediately he smiles, his body relaxes and the contained energy opens up and reaches out. You can see and feel a sudden aliveness, a new state of being arising out of the connecting resonance.

We know this shift of state from our own experience. Do you feel and act the same way when alone as with a friend or lover? Are you exactly the same person when you spend time with your family at the holidays as during the work week? Relationship evokes something new in us. This is true not just for contact with people. An inner shift happens whenever we connect deeply with anyone or anything.

A client was coming out of a difficult session of hypnosis distressed and disoriented. I needed to help her return to a normal state before she could walk out of the office and drive home. Just then the little dog in her car outside started barking. I remarked on it and she looked out. Her face lit up, immediately full of life. "Look at him, the little love," she said, "He knows I'm up here. He's telling me it's time to come down." In a few moments she was ready to leave. That loving contact had pulled her back into herself, helped her reconnect.

Relationship and the Heart

As humans we are born with an organ of connection. This is the heart, the seat of emotions and feelings. The heart does not lie, we do not feel without being related in some way.

Feelings are the mirror of connection, they reflect the strength and nature of relatedness. Like a voltmeter, the heart measures the charge, the movement of energy, the power and vitality of connection. We know the resulting measure, the readout, through the quality of our emotions. If there is no feeling there is no relationship, the connection is insubstantial. If the charge is hot and high, whether burning love or boiling hate, the binding force is intense and powerful.

Fear, anger and sadness are just as related as affection. The polarity is simply different. We push away what is frightening. We attack whatever angers us. We cling to the loss that saddens us. All feeling is a movement of the heart. Most strongly, we move toward whatever we wish for and love.

Love

What is love? Love is the sacred essence of connection joining heaven and earth, as Plato tells us. It is the connecting energy of the universe, a dimension of the Life Force. Our own personal experience of love, whatever form it takes, is this universal binding force compressed into our limited being. When we love, we create a little more connection and wholeness.

This is the sacred intention of the suggestions Sharon Saltzberg offers us in her book, *Loving Kindness*.[5] She invites us to practice *metta*, the Buddhist word for boundless compassion. The same exact advice is given to us by Christian mystics and Islamic Sufis alike.[6] When we open up our hearts to all beings, to all experiences of connection, we align ourselves with universal Love.

Without practice our hearts do not expand enough to experience this unbounded energy. Our personal liking, affections, attractions and passions are more or less distorted or diluted

177

reflections of universal Love. In our ordinary hearts we can feel a mere trickle of the real power. This power catches us at its most impetuous when we 'fall in love.'

More has been written about romantic love and sexual attraction than any other topic. It is the stuff of poetry, popular songs, movies and great plays. Yet from a psychological viewpoint, it remains a crazy anomaly. Everyone needs to experience, at least once, the overwhelming power of losing oneself to another person. A developmental crisis of the heart, falling in love cracks open our hidden alienation and selfishness and allows the universe to flood in. It is not rational or sane, but, like a dangerous doorway, it leads into another possibility of being.

David confessed, after the third date, that he feared he was falling in love again. He hardly knew the woman and yet he felt obsessed by her, totally submerged, and it was worrying him. Too often in the past his relationships had turned bitter and painful. He asked me, "What should I do? Should I cool it off, be careful, slow it all down. Or should I continue to see her and let it happen? I don't want it to turn out like the others."

When faced with this question I often respond in the same way: *'Falling in love' is a gift that you can hardly afford to refuse. Experience it as deeply as you are able, knowing it is time limited and not the same as 'being in love.' It brings with it a tremendous shaking up of your deepest self, an unusual goodness and selflessness that will amaze you, terrible doubts and anguish at the thought of rejection and an overwhelming urge to merge with the loved one. The deeper process has you in its grip. You might as well accept you have little choice but to enjoy the terrifying and exhilarating ride.*

Of all the meter-readings of the heart that confuse most, romantic love comes top. Falling in love is the ultimate attempt at connectedness, a wish to abandon separateness in favor of a greater union, an urge to bond and blend with the beloved. It has such power and takes so many forms that it is easy to be bewildered.

Often the urge to connect is confused with connection itself. Then we are in love with love itself. Our heart seems to say that we feel deeply for the other person but is, in truth, simply reading the strength of our own yearning. Unrequited love is not true connection. We are trying to open up our hearts to more connection. Many 'failed' relationships are preparation for a mutual loving connection in the future. They are attempts to heal our damaged hearts.

Connection and Family

We learn connection from the pattern of relationship in our first family. Here our hearts were invited to open, or forced to close; here we were hurt or healed. The relational habits of our family are deeply embedded in our psyche.

Were you welcomed, accepted and adored without reservation, just because you were you? Was there a vitality, a loving flow of conversation, enough attention to go round when you sat down together for a family meal? Do you feel a profound unbreakable connection to your siblings—a deep respect and gratitude for your parents? If you do, you are extremely fortunate and blessed—and part of a minority.

Our families are mostly disappointing. To the child's unconscious, parents are God-like numinous beings who hold our physical and psychic well-being in their hands. Ordinary men and women struggle to live up to this archetypal ideal and usually fall short. We all experience a subtle sense of loss because of the imperfection of our parents. Deeper within we know they should be flawless, totally caring and accepting. We expect their love to be unconditional and transcendent.

But it doesn't happen. We are saddled with fallible parents and we, in turn, become imperfect caregivers to our own offspring. All mothers and fathers fall short, sometimes dreadfully. However much we love them, however much we appreciate their care and concern, it is hard to pardon parental failings. The sad truth is that our childhood connection with our parents sets the imperfect pattern for our own adult relationships.

A dream: *David is visiting his old home. He doesn't recognize it; his parents have been remodeling and the house seems sterile, empty and cold. Other people are milling around but David feels out of place and uncomfortable. No one talks to him except his father who keeps showing off what they have done to the house. David cannot seem to get away. Then inexplicably, he finds himself wandering off down the driveway.*

The dream is telling David that he is no longer at home with the old parental patterns. He doesn't belong in their world. It is empty, like the cold relationship between his mother and father that still centers around things and activities, not intimacy. He is struggling to get free, to find his own way. As he begins a new relationship, he has to remember not to fall into the traps set by his upbringing. It is easy for him to keep his feelings hidden, to stay distant. Yet if he does, he may find himself trapped in an empty, loveless partnership.

The influence of those two frail and imperfect beings, our parents, is, for good or ill, imprinted on every one of our intimate relationships. We cannot escape this influence but we can shape it into a new and benevolent form. As we strive to become more connected, more loving, more intimately involved with our lives, we modify the patterns that kept us separate. This is the journey of relationship, a lengthy project that is one of the central tasks of psychotherapy.

Therapeutic Relationship

Why do people come to psychotherapy? What are they looking for? The simple answer is *relationship*—a safe, healing, intimate alliance with another human being. When a client settles in the chair opposite me and we begin to speak, to relate, something happens. It is not in what we talk about. It is not specifically in me or in that other person. Some possibility that did not exist before is being created by our being together.

Counseling theory calls this something a "therapeutic relationship," the intimate collaboration of client and therapist that is therapy. More important than technique or skill, the quality of this connection is what allows a client to feel safe enough to change. Carl Rogers, the originator of non-directive counseling, gave us a map of the basic elements of this healing relationship: *undemanding love, acceptance, respect, trust.* These form "unconditional positive regard," the heart of therapy.[7]

In transpersonal psychotherapy we talk about these healing aspects as creating the *therapeutic container,* a sacred connection of two people that invites the power of the Greater process to be present.[8] This form of relationship is the most intense vehicle for the deepest human healing. The intention is to relinquish control of what happens to some greater power, so it necessarily entails a willingness for both client and therapist to be unsettled, to take a risk. The transpersonal process is not directed by our minds or technique, it is 'chaotic.' The result can never be totally predicted.[9]

Laurel was the first client who taught me about the turbulence of the therapeutic relationship. I was working in a psychology department in England, a few years out of training. The receptionist whispered a nervous warning about the client sitting quietly in the communal waiting room. I went out to meet the young woman with short dark hair and hidden eyes rimmed with black.

It was a bitterly cold winter day, yet she was dressed in jeans and a skimpy black tank top. Beside her was a heavily laden, worn cloth bag. Except for her face and palms of the hands, most of her visible skin was covered in tattoos. There were skulls and roses, blood-dripping daggers, necklaces and bracelets, mythical beasts and curlicues rippling across her shoulders, chest, back and arms. Even her bare feet showed designs through the thong sandals.

Seeking Wholeness

I saw Laurel off and on for three years. For most of the first year, she appeared on time, never made eye contact and hardly spoke. I struggled to connect, to find the real person behind the tattooed mask. Every technique, every trick of silence, suggestion, question, and soliloquy, seemed futile. As I gave up trying so hard, ever so slowly, she began to emerge.

Over the following months, I would occasionally catch a glimpse of a frightened little girl peeking out from under a fringe of hair. The mascara rimmed eyes hid a well of pain from early abuse and abandonment.

At the bottom of her cloth bag nestled the symbols of Laurel's terror—a lethal pocketknife and a hammerhead in a sock. She had once stabbed a man who was attracted to her and followed her home . As she put it, "I didn't want to hurt him, he was a nice guy. But he just kept at me. I had no choice. I felt trapped. I cannot be trapped."

That was true. A small wild animal with sharp teeth, she could never tolerate the confinement of intimacy. The early therapy sessions were torture. She did not know how to escape the therapy room. My questions and subtle demands kept pinning her down— more traps. Like that little animal, underneath she was soft and vulnerable.

As she relaxed into our relationship, her dependence on me grew—another trap. She became more anxious. Without notice, she inexplicably did not appear for her normal appointment. The intuitive connection between us was strong enough for me to know something was terribly wrong.

I eventually found her apartment. After knocking for ages, she groggily let me in, dressed in fabulous, flowing costume. There, in the middle of the living room floor, was an equally fantastical arrangement of feathers, flowers, rich draperies and cushions. It was her funeral bier. She had lain down and taken a bottle of analgesics. Fortunately, it was not enough and she recovered after a short hospital stay.

The therapeutic ride got rougher. As she stopped being depressed, her ambivalence grew. It was our connection, and not what I did or said, that was making the difference, both healing the childhood scars and terrifying her. I was feeling over-involved, experiencing the backwash of her inner turmoil. My supervision group muttered disapproval—I did not have enough distance or objectivity. They were right. I, like Laurel, was learning to connect deeply, to feel the power of relationship in ways I never had known. It was wild, intense and very real.

It did not end tidily. My learning curve was slow and I had not realized the depth of her fear of intimacy. She decided to stop therapy abruptly. At our last session she appeared decisive and strong, immediately telling me, "I can't have you be so important to me. You'll leave eventually and I'll be worse off. So I'm ending it here and now."

She made a strange request, "Please do one last thing for me. Stand up, close your eyes and say nothing." Puzzled, I complied. She surrounded me with a circle of salt to magically neutralize my power over her, handed me the book I had lent her and left. I never saw her again. I think of her sometimes with a twinge of regret and hope she has learned to love without dread.

Laurel taught strong lessons: *Never underestimate the power of relationship. Relationship has the power to hurt or heal, to create or destroy. It is a risk to be involved, connected and vulnerable to another person. Yet when we are damaged, made smaller through relationship, it is through relationship and connection that we can become whole.*

Psychotherapy is a 'stripped down' version of a loving relationship. It provides intimacy, respect and attention without the intrusion of sex and over involvement. We all unconsciously seek a therapeutic relationship for our unmet needs, for all the injuries of our earlier experiences. This is exactly what we need and exactly what gets us into trouble. In many failed relationships we are trying to get emotional sustenance from the wrong place, from a depleted source.

Psychotherapy provides a relatively safe place to test out the turbulent waters of relationship. It is not an end in itself or an alternative to deep intimacy. When it works, we are more able to reach out to others in our lives. We learn to put relationship into practice. We learn to love others and ourselves deeply and without holding back.[10]

Connecting to Ourselves

Love is the path to integration. Fear of humiliation and rejection are the main obstacles. As we shield our vulnerability behind its many protective layers, we keep separate and emotionally isolated. It is difficult to push through the shadow of fear and resentment. It can seem like an impossible task. Learning to love without reservation is a life-long undertaking that takes immense commitment and courage.

We first need to tolerate our own shortcomings, this is the beginnings of love. The shadow of critical judgement hangs over much of what we think and do. Probably you know that part of you that keeps up a negative running commentary. What you probably do not recognize is that it is really trying to keep you safe. The inner critic does all it can to avoid the humiliation of making mistakes, but in doing so, it also makes impossible demands.[11]

We cannot live up to unrealistic and unreachable ideals. We always fall short. The resulting self-attack creates a searing tear in our being and befogs our ability to see the goodness in others. When we open our hearts to acceptance and self-forgiveness, the critical inner voice can, at last, become quieter.

At the same time, we cannot simply ignore our failings. Like a familiar frayed rug, we get used to the broken threads of our personality and we overlook the lose ends and ragged patches. Our blind spots, weaknesses and selfishness keep us stuck and disconnected. Unless we see, with pristine clarity, how we really are, there is no way to begin the long task of mending. This is real self love.

Elizabeth's children had grown and left but were in regular contact. She shared the large house with her quiet husband, life had a regular routine. Her life was settled, yet she still felt troubled. Years of therapy and a strong inner life had honed her sensibilities. The childhood hurts from a self-centered and controlling mother seemed resolved, but still something remained incomplete.

One session, Elizabeth brought in a particularly vivid dream: *I am with some men. There is a subtle sense of threat as if the men had killed someone in the past. Yet nothing is out of the ordinary and I am having fun being the center of attention. One of the men takes me secretly aside and tells me of a plot to murder me. He says I must get away immediately and go to the mountains for safety.*

Elizabeth was disturbed by the dream, yet the message was clear and simple: she should withdraw into her own inner space for a period. Not to do so was dangerous.

The dream initiated a difficult time for her. Over the next months another layer of her small self was stripped away. She began to see how she subtly manipulated her children and husband to get the attention she desperately craved. Recognizing her own self-centeredness, so like her mother's, was harrowing.

It took immense courage for Elizabeth to look herself in the face and find herself wanting. Most of us push away those parts of ourselves that we don't want to see. Passion, sensitivity and sensuality as well as selfishness, may have been unacceptable to the adults of our childhood. Now those qualities are entombed, an undiscovered and fearful dark place in our being.

Do you wonder how other people experience you—whether they see your private anxieties and shameful habits? Do you accept yourself unconditionally? Can you face and then forgive your own stupidity, mistakes and meanness, knowing you will be more aware in future?

We have to inhabit our own being, there is no alternative. We cannot be who we are not. Accepting who we are and connecting to all aspects of our humanness, we begin to rehabilitate even the most shadowy and dark aspects of our soul.

Connecting to the Shadow

Meeting our shadow is disturbing.[12] It forces us to face those aspects of our personality that make us squirm with discomfort. We are so used to looking only at our 'good' side that the shadow lurks dark and creepy behind us. Neglected and hidden, it is all that we avoid and refuse to own. Projected, the shadow becomes what we envy, hate or wish to destroy in others.

In a dreamgroup, a woman shared a dream: *she was in the ocean and a dark man attacked her with an axe, chopping her into pieces.* I suggested that we invite the energy of the axe-murderer into the group to own it and feel it. There was a deathly silence as a lurking menace filled the room. Suddenly, a scared and angry man burst out, "That's not a good thing to do. I won't do it." In resisting my suggestion, he protected himself and the group from experiencing the darkness and terror of the shadow.

It is hard to own the shadowy axe-murderer within. The idea is so foreign to our laundered view of ourselves. Yet there is always some situation where we could lose self control, even Jesus got angry and violent with the merchants in the temple. When we are less than we think we should be—cruel, impatient, selfish and manipulative—we either wallow in guilt or quickly expunge it from awareness. Neither strategy helps in the long run. Unless we actually accept that all those demons are part of who we are, unless we connect in deeply to that level of our being, we miss the opportunity to change.

This society prefers that we kill or lock away forever those who disturb our complacency: molesters, murders, drug dealers and thieves. It is comfortable to have the shadow of our culture consigned to oblivion. Then we know for certain they are not like us, not ordinary people, but deformed and dangerous monsters. What if they are human? What if they are you and me? Should we murder them, lock them in confinement until they go crazy?

All of us dream of murder, mayhem and forbidden acts, remembered or not. During one period of intense change, I dreamed nightly of having sex with different members of my family, both male and female.[13] I was taken aback. Even knowing the symbolic nature of dreams it was still disturbing. The final dream was the most bizarre: *I had both male and female genitals and was sexually united with my brother whose organs were exactly complementary.*

With distance, I am grateful for those dreams. They invited me to accept even the most shameful parts of my experience as real and important. In dreams, the sexual act often reflects the orgasmic intensity of connecting with parts of ourselves that have been lost and separated. It is about becoming whole, not simply about gratification. Our society cheapens sex, does not recognize it as a sacred manifestation of the Life Force. We are obsessed by or ashamed of our sexual nature. So sex and sexuality get stuffed down into the cultural shadow with the rest of the baggage.

The cultural shadow keeps large chunks of our experience obscured beneath a blanket of ignorance and self deception. We do not want to face or feel the suffering we impose on each other and the world. Our comfortable life incurs a trail of unnoticed death and destruction: trees are cut down to make our houses; the earth is penetrated, polluted and torn to service the wonders of technology; animals and plants give their lives to provide food and a million convenient products. While we grow rich and fat, others starve. This also is our forgotten dark side.

Recognizing the shadow jolts our view of the world, it call us to a new awareness. I remember a simple event that extinguished my enjoyment of the hunt. From the age of eleven or twelve it was natural for us boys to carry a shotgun into my grandfather's woods

187

in search of game. It turned sour on me suddenly one ordinary day when I shot a gray squirrel out of a tree. It lay wounded and struggling, waiting for me to end its life with a quick twist of its neck. I saw the fear and pain in its eyes, felt the spark of connection between two living beings. Then I killed it. Instantly there was no pleasure, no point to its death. I had senselessly robbed it of that which is most precious—life.

Later, I lived and worked on a farm and death of an animal took on a different meaning. One soggy day, I helped deliver three kids to my sister's old nanny goat, Egeltina. The last was tiny and premature, its hoofs still translucent slivers of gelatin. We took it in beside the turf fire and nursed it to health. It grew to be a boisterous billy and one day it was ready for the pot.

Killing a billy goat is no small task. It clings to life with every fiber of its being, kicking and struggling. More aware of the import of taking a life, I tried to approach the task with gratitude and patience. Becoming intimately involved in the sacrifice, in the mystery of dying, consecrates the act. Even in taking life, if we stay connected, death can be sacred.[14] That is how we rehabilitate that which is dark, by filling our experience with the light of awareness.

The same applies to our own death. Most often our own extinction is a forgotten unreality that we push off into the distant future. Seldom do we imagine our dying as an ultimately blessed experience for which our whole life is preparation. If we are taken unprepared and incomplete, what does that say about the meaning of our life? It is as if we knit a scarf but forget to cast off and the pattern unravels. Looking back over your life from the perspective of your deathbed, will you be truly satisfied? Can you live each day conscious of your inevitable demise?[15]

Death is the ultimate teacher whose lessons we need to learn while yet alive. It tells us that everything ends, nothing is forever, we must "seize the day." To be vitally alive on the journey toward our death invites us to connect completely with each moment, to meet each experience as it comes. This is the spiritual purpose of being embodied, for a time, in this world.

Connecting to the Natural World

We live in an increasingly secular society, yet the paradox is that while many people actively reject formal religion, more and more consider themselves to be on a spiritual path. Unlike bygone eras when formal religious institutions had a spiritual monopoly, today increasing numbers find serenity through immersion in nature.

Do you spend time in the natural world? Do you find yourself craving the quiet of a forest or the freshness of green open space? Have you wondered what it is that makes a hike in the country special and different from walking city streets?

There is a magical energy emanating from the natural landscape. Millions of acres of national parks, state forest and protected wilderness attest to the growing realization of the preciousness of those parts of the earth where human impact is curtailed. The wish to feel an ecological connection with nature reflects our urge toward wholeness. We see the trees, but more deeply, we resonate to the forest, the connected whole, dimly sensing the "web of life" from which we have become estranged.

It does not require the grandeur of the Rockies to feel a connection to living things. I am a gardener, and gardeners everywhere know the joy of coaxing a house plant to verdant health, of seeing the bulbs bloom in the spring, of eating your own vegetables. Creating just the right environment of soil, water and light for a fragile seedling is a powerful symbol for our own development. When I lived in England, my garden was miniscule. Yet it spoke to me of the mystery of life.

We all can invite the natural world into our lives. Trees, grass and flowers are never far away, even in the midst of the city. I have a respectful relationship with that elderly ponderosa pine near my hogan. Do you know a particular tree intimately? They too are beings.

All of us children, young and old, spontaneously pick up and take home interesting natural objects. We feel their wild magic. Those rocks, pinecones, shells and feathers that grace our shelves are informal altars to sacred nature. The earth has always been a Goddess. She requires our respectful devotion. We are beginning to recollect what was obvious to our ancestors that all humanity is intimately connected to a great natural being that is Gaia, the spirit of our planet.[16] If we neglect or mistreat her, she may shrug us off like offending parasites.

The stars above us look down on our delicate world, a uniquely bountiful globe sailing in a vast sea of darkness. Can we feel the earth, alive with billions upon billions of organisms, all connected and breathing together? We too are natural organisms. Can we inhale and exhale to the slow rhythm of nature? When we are still and aware, there is always a vibration in the depths of our being. We know and sense the Life Force flowing through everything.

George Leonard expresses this sensibility beautifully:

At the heart of each of us, whatever our imperfections, there exists a silent pulse of perfect rhythm, a complex of wave forms and resonances, which is absolutely individual and unique, and yet which connects us to everything in the universe. The act of getting in touch with this pulse can transform our personal experience and in some way alter the world around us.[17]

The Presence of Wholeness

Wholeness is not a final state to be achieved, it is an ever unfolding process. Each pine seed is whole, relatively self-contained and complete. Yet the tree that grows from that seed, that connects to earth, sun, air, insects and life all around is so much more. It embodies a greater wholeness. We are all seeds waiting to burst into a fuller life.

Every moment we have to decide to make the effort to connect more deeply, let go of separateness and surrender to the greater whole. Is this challenge worth accepting? When we look at those who rise to this challenge we see a radiant *presence*, one that is deeply related.

I spent one Christmas at Port Glenone monastery in Northern Ireland. Each morning, at three A.M., I would wake for vigils. As I sat with the monks in the choir, I could feel the chant echo through my being, feel the inner meaning of 'Joy and Peace.'

Dom Aengus was abbot, the elected spiritual director of the monastery. A white-haired, ruddy featured man in his late fifties, he sparkled with love and enthusiasm. You could feel him enter a room. His presence went before him like an energy wave, creating a space of acceptance and brightness.

After the holiday I asked Dom Aengus if I could visit my friend Brother Veder who was living in a hermitage further north. He smiled with his twinkling eyes as he told me: Brother Veder had made a vow of solitude and so Dom Aengus, as his spiritual father, could not give permission for Veder to see anyone. "However," he went on in a soft brogue, "If you should just happen to pass by and visit, what could I do about it!" He silently wrote and handed me a page of detailed directions to the remote cottage.

The ability to respond directly and lovingly to the spirit of the moment without regard for rules or form, is the mark of a true human being. Dom Aengus could be present without pettiness or self-interest getting in the way. The energy of his shadow had merged into wholeness. When with him, I too felt an invitation to become whole.

Winifred Rushforth also had a quality of being fully herself. At ninety five, with nothing to prove, she had much wisdom to share. Fifty years as a therapist left her ever-more excited and appreciative of the human soul. Her welcomes were rich and loving, always personal and accepting of whoever arrived. There was no pretense of knowledge, no need to say the right word.

Winifred would preside over her dreamgroups with a quiet and attentive presence, occasionally commenting or telling a story sparked by the dream. Her stories were invariably about the transcendent connectivity and meaningfulness of life and relationship. Everything made sense in some greater loving context.

If we ask, "How do I become a Gandhi, Dom Aengus or Winifred?" we ask the wrong question. The real question is, "How do I become more completely myself?" One thing is obvious when you meet someone who embodies wholeness—there is nothing bland or homogenized about their presence. They are completely alive and individual. While totally themselves they are yet surrendered to some Greater principle. This is a paradox of the spiritual life—to be fully yourself, and simultaneously an integral part of the vast interconnected whole.

William McNamara, Abbot of Crestone monastery, describes this paradox beautifully:

> We must get off the surface, away from the periphery, and move into the center where the fire is, and there become consumed by the fire and really become alive. Aliveness is the first effect of living a disciplined life. We must all become disciplined wild people. That's the spiritual life. You participate in the life of the spirit— the spirit of God. God has no boundaries and no limitations. He's infinitely wild![18]

Do you want to be fully alive? Are you willing to give up certainty, security and comfort to embrace the wildness of a spiritual life? Do you have the discipline to keep striving toward wholeness even when it seems impossible? Can you let go of who you think you are and surrender your idea of separateness? These are difficult challenges faced by all on the spiritual journey. Thankfully, we do not have to face them without guidance.

Invoking Presence

Great teachers over thousands of years tell us there is help available. Whether it comes from our own inner nature or from some external force is irrelevant. We open ourselves to the Divine, to the boundlessness of the Greater process, to that which is beyond our limited self. This is the essence of prayer and contemplation. It may be a beseeching, a thankfulness, a cry of pain, a moment of joy. It could be a verbal formula, a formless inner movement, an ocean of emptiness—but it is always an attempt to connect with something greater. Contemplative prayer invokes the *presence of wholeness.*

I went to a Catholic school where the Rosary, the Stations of the Cross, the "Our Father" were familiar repetitive formulae that tugged at the robe of Mary, Jesus and even God Himself, trying to get benevolent attention. As a child, they were magical incantations that would somehow change the world and make it right. Now, seeing Tibetan monks and Sufis fingering their beads reminds me of the nuns with their Rosaries. All are embodying a universal spiritual truth.

Prayer calms the mind, directs it away from distraction and helps us remember. The *Jesus Prayer* of the Eastern Orthodox Church, the *dhikr* of Islam, the recent Catholic movement of *Centering Prayer* and ancient Hindu mantras are all means to invite a sacred Presence.[19] Words and religious iconography are less important than the intention of constantly directing attention towards the transcendent.[20]

We tend to only pray at particular times, if at all. Prayer is reserved for church, the Sabbath or when we want something. This is a strange way of relating to the transpersonal as though it is bound by our schedule. True prayer has no timetable. We can be prayerfully aware while we drive, when we are on hold on the phone, when we are going for a walk. We can even learn to invite that Presence when we are working or deep in conversation. It matters little whether we call it *mindfulness* or the "Practice of the Presence of God," we are creating space for something Greater.[21]

Through prayer, meditation and ritual we attempt to reach beyond ourselves. Yet we have no power to command that sublime Presence. Our spiritual practices are like traps set to ensnare sunlight. The strange wonder is that they do anything at all. Maybe they have results because the traps are made of sunlight and we are made of sunlight and the sunlight wishes to be caught. The Divine, the transcendent, is not separate from us or from the universe. It is present in all the flow and connectivity of creation.

When the transpersonal illuminates our experience, it comes as an effortless inflowing of grace, a lightness and completeness of being, sudden joy and humor, unexpected healing, a sense of knowing a greater reality. Whatever its form, it is always new and unexpected, like a breath of fresh and cool air that enlivens a sullen day. It proclaims that we are all involved in a sacred endeavor to produce a little more connection and wholeness in the universe.

CHAPTER 9

Finding Our Way

◎ ☀ 🔔

In order to arrive at what you do not know
 You must go by a way which is the way of ignorance.
In order to possess what you do not possess
 You must go by the way of dispossession.
In order to arrive at what you are not
 You must go through the way in which you are not.
And what you do not know is the only thing you know
And what you own is what you do not own
And where you are is where you are not.
—T. S. Eliot (from *East Coker*)

Life flows swiftly and we are swept along. I remember the tidal power, the gigantic force that propelled our tiny sailing craft out to sea when my father, brother and I were 'ship-wrecked.' The current was irresistible, all we could do was let go and trust. We were at the mercy of an energy that took us with it, whether we wanted or not. Such is the flow of life.

So how are we to find our way in the face of this torrent? We must become more present, more aware and more fully connected with all aspects of our experience. Small and impermanent as we are, we have to live with exuberance, make every minute count. We can't withdraw and shield ourselves from the risk of involvement, yet we can't be attached either. It is all immensely important but we must stay free of entanglements. Life demands a passionate response, a passion that is impassionate, a deep connection that does not cling, a love free of desire.

Embracing Impermanence

By the time I was twenty five my first young 'love', Mary-Jane, and my best childhood friend, Conrad, had both died in different auto accidents. John, another friend from kindergarten, was dying from a neurological disease. I learned, through unavoidable loss, that everything is impermanent. Yet I also realized that there is no place for despair or avoidance. Life is most precious because it is so fragile and fleeting.

Change is constant and death awaits. It is all around us, in the animals and plants we eat, in the transition of the seasons, in the crises that fill the news. Death is a reality that accompanies life, side by side, light and shadow. It tells us there is no avoiding the inevitable rhythm of process, the beginning and ending of everything. We may try to clutch on to material security, grab ahold of valued parts of our being, attempt to recapture 'good' experiences, but it will all be taken from us. Like a little boy holding on to the skirt of his mother on the first day of school, eventually we have to let go.

Here is a dream that occasionally appears near the beginning of therapy: *I am stuck with a dead body and don't know where to hide it. Somehow I am implicated in the death—maybe I murdered the person. Now I have to get rid of the evidence, bury it or dump it, before the police come and find me.*

This dream confesses the difficulty we have letting go of extinct and burdensome parts of our personality. We stay attached, dragging decaying entities around with us looking for a place to put them. It is not right and we know we are guilty of avoiding change, but yet we cling. Only as we accept our shadows, become our own confessor, give up pretense of perfection can we be liberated.

Life demands that we move on. There is no time to stay stuck, circling the same tired byways. We have to recognize the dead weight that drags us down and notice the patterns that keep recurring and recycling. They tell us where to start. Open up, let go and allow the vitality of the Life Force to fill you. The burden will become lighter.

Experience is transient. We cannot cocoon our frailty in a sticky web of attachment or build our self-esteem on transitory accomplishments. Even spiritual experience comes and goes. One morning, rising early to walk the wooded parklands of Port Glenone Monastery, I was taken by a sense of awe at the perfection and connectedness of nature. I felt at one, perfectly fitted to that moment in time and space.

A devious part of my ego decided that I was now transformed, that I could hold and keep this perfect state.[1] Describing the experience to a friend, he burst my bubble of self-importance saying, "God gives you a glimpse of how you could be. Don't confuse that with how you are. You still have to bring that way of being into reality." We are always in process of becoming. We have never arrived.

When we accept the ephemeral and evolving nature of all experiences, life becomes richer and more complex. The future is obscured around the next bend, the past is already gone. The terrain of the journey unfolds around and within us as we travel through life.

Take a few moments to stop and notice where you are. Let go of the busyness in your mind and body. Remember the years you have lived, the hopes and dreams that have been and vanished. What is there to hold on to? If you strip away the surface desires, what is left? Can you live now, be aware of yourself only in this moment?

Noticing and accepting ourselves in every instant intensifies each new sight and sound, every thought and feeling. The moving, rising wave of the present lifts and carries us. Our experience deepens.

Enriching Experience

We live bathed in a sea of experience. We have to make sense of everything, find where it fits, decide what it means. Thus we create the magical and mysterious connections that are meanings.

Meaning is not fixed. Everything we think, feel and do is woven into the fabric of our being. Who you are now, your process, is an unfinished tapestry on the loom of life. The overall pattern, the design keeps shifting as another colored thread of experience is added. You are constantly changing and the meaning of your life changes with you.

We have to deepen experience, make it richer and more meaningful. The older I get, the more I feel, sense and appreciate. Life is gradually stripping away the worn and tired banality and adding a rainbow of colors. I remind myself to notice the transient beauty of the morning glories, to take just a few moments to give my son a hug in the morning. Each client requires that I become just a little more present, enter in a little more deeply. I connect to a source of illuminating energy and in my eyes the office is flooded with inexplicable light.

Experience is our creation. Any sensation can be one-dimensional, shallow and flat, or eloquent and vibrant. It depends on how we answer the questions life asks us. Are you willing to take the risk to feel more? There is always more, much more than meets the eye and meets the mind.

The materialist sees only the physical surface of life, the sensualist feels only the texture. Yet life has rich and many-layered strata. Like archeologists, as we dig beneath the surface, we discover unexpected treasures. Everything we touch with minds or hands becomes imbued with a numinous vibrancy. These are the jewels of our deeper self.

Think of a dream that stays with you. Turn it over in your mind to discover the light refracted from its many facets. Appreciate its strange beauty, the images and associations it evokes. What is this obscure creation, luminous with meaning? It is a gift, a message, a bauble offered to your awareness from somewhere deeper within. I learned this indelibly during one year, 1979, in Edinburgh, Scotland.

Once a week, Orianne and I would walk across town to the solidly built Victorian house where Winifred Rushforth lived. It was our night for dreamgroup. As we came in, Winifred would be sitting in her armchair, wrinkled face glowing in a halo of white hair. She would beckon each person to the group in a peculiarly Scottish way, "Come away, come away and join us."

With eight other assorted people, huddled around an electric heater, we would drink weak Lapsang Souchong tea and tell our dreams. There was no time for social pleasantries. We hardly knew the ordinary lives of the other participants, yet we came to know them far more intimately through their dream-life.

Winifred would sit quietly while we shared responses to each person's dream. Occasionally she would tell a rambling story or interject some pointed comment. I remember a timid spinster telling the group about a dream in which she, "had intercourse with the devil." Winifred looked intently over her glasses, her white hair haloed around her head, and asked, "Do you mean he fucked you?"

Mostly she allowed the flow of the group to find its own course. We were embarked on a sacred mission to discover the riches of our nightly experience.

Years later, I am still filled with the spirit of that group. Winifred led us to the entrance of another world. She opened a treasure of unexpected meaning that enriched us all and engendered a boundless trust in the workings of the deeper Self.

There is no doubt in my mind of the profound guidance inscribed in every dream.

Dreaming our Lives

Dreams are not simply interesting. They are sacred messages from the depths, sent to guide us, to show us how to approach life. That guidance is not only in the images or stories, it is the fabric of the dreaming. All experience, whether of sleep or waking, is symbolic, visionary and filled with meaning.

You may have heard the famous story of the Taoist sage, Chuang Tsu and the butterfly:

Once upon a time, I Chuang Tsu, dreamed I was a butterfly flying happily here and there, enjoying life without knowing who I was. Suddenly I woke up and I was indeed Chuang Tsu. Did Chuang Tsu dream he was a butterfly, or did the butterfly dream he was Chuang Tsu?[2]

Life is a dreaming. Our whole existence is a domain of symbolic meaning no more or less real to our deeper self than a dream. Our ego thinks it is in charge but in reality it is being carried by invisible helpers. To understand any happening deeply we approach it as a 'big' dream. Every action, every outer event, is a motif in a visionary narrative that tells of our being.

In our dreams, as in myths and fairy tales, all travelling, every footstep, is part of the "Great Journey" of life.[3] Cars, buses and trains are not just modes of transport, but symbolic ways of moving through the world. Are you driving or are you driven? Houses are not simply structures of habitation but reflections of the Self. You may know well the living room of your personality but have you gone down to see what lurks in the basement?

If we inhabit our outer life from the standpoint of dreaming, we find an unexpected richness. Say you are driving along a street and a bird flies into your windshield causing you to swerve. Is this a random meaningless event? To find out, ask yourself the question: "If this were a dream, what would it mean?" Maybe you are moving too fast, too unaware through your life and your spirit is being run down.

To approach events as if in a dream allows you to experience life and its meaning in a different way. You invite the deeper significance to rise to the surface.

Living our life within the symbolic adds a dimension that is difficult to articulate. We dig deeper into the essence of everything. We expand our hearts and minds into the whole of life, into the whole of human existence. Things are not what they seem or what we assume, they have greater import than we realize.

To invite a richer meaning into our lives connects all levels of our being, including those that make us uneasy. The resulting friction and paradox evoke new and innovative solutions to the questions posed by life. We begin to see and feel it all from the most superficial to the most profound. As it all fits together into a new pattern of wholeness, we unexpectedly awaken.

Awakening

A memory: I am walking along the Cork road just South of Dungarvan. It is spring in Ireland with a softness to the air and a green to the grass that is exquisite. The road is flat and straight after lifting out of town for a few miles with a single wire fence beside me and some scrubby oak trees across the way. In the distance, the road follows the contours of the land, rolling in long waves of asphalt and hedges of bright yellow furze. Just ahead is a tiny abandoned brick schoolhouse, upright and austere. Clouds are scudding in a watery, blue gray sky, trying to decide whether to drench me again. It is quiet, with the gentle emptiness of few people and things.

Sixteen, recently fired from my job as bartender in the Hotel Ormond, I am on my way to seek my fortune in the big city of Cork. In my pocket are a few Irish pounds, large colorful bank notes with the smiling faces of the Old Irish River Gods. Filled with unspoken feelings, inexplicit longings and strange apprehensions, I am mostly hoping that the next car will give me a ride.

Somehow I awake, reach awareness of myself and where I am in that moment, "I am me and this is my life." Disconnected thoughts fill my adolescent mind, yet deeper within resides a sense of knowing. The moment captures me piercing through my small self into a greater reality. I feel a subtle presence that tells me all is, and will be, well. I am free, no ties, no responsibilities and my heart is light within my chest, anything could happen. The road unfolds before me like the possibilities of my young life.

Are you awake? Look around and notice yourself, where you are now. Can you feel the texture of your own awareness, the essence of your aliveness? We are called to wakefulness, to being mindful of each moment.[4] If we but arouse from our drowsiness, become aware of who we are, immeasurable possibilities await.

We all have times of flawless, full awareness. Then we know and have a sense of the import of our life and a connection with its meaning. These are not usually extraordinary flashes of enlightenment, they are just the ordinary wonder and wondering that comes from being alive. The voices of children playing in the distance, a captivating piece of music, an intense conversation, an insightful book or movie all bring a brightening of our sense of self. We are remembering who we are.

Remembering

I remember waking in a room of my own on a Sunday morning in my grandmother's cottage. The fresh linen sheets felt cool on my body and I could hear a chorus of a hundred birds outside my window. I had all the luxurious time in the world to gather myself together before the day began.

We are called to remember, to cross the threshold of mindfulness, capture the moment, and invite illumination into our soul. As we re-collect all our parts, all our *members*, we begin to remember. We are gathering together the whole of who we are.

Remembering takes practice, the constant directing of awareness to what is most essential. Pay attention to the center of yourself, that place from which experience flows. You begin to sense who you are, feel the Life Force flowing through your being. Now you begin to resonate with the flux of the universe, take another small step toward a Self that is nameless and unlimited.

How are we to remember when forgetting is so easy? Begin by recognizing the quality of your experience. Remind yourself that you are alive, here and now, and it is time to awake. Anything can help—a simple written memo, quiet breaks during the day, a run or hike in nature, the harmonious arrangement of a room that invokes serenity. All these and more can be invitations to return to a greater sense of Self.

Consider carefully who you decide to be with. Unconsciousness is catching. If you are constantly with people who have forgotten, it is easy to fall into a similar forgetting. Surround yourself with loving people. Being in community with those who are fully present helps you remember.

Regular spiritual practice, a routine of prayer, meditation or devotion, gives structure and definition to awareness. Make the practice simple and natural so it fits seamlessly into your life. Spirituality does not require thought or strategy. Have your practice become an unthinking part of every day, there always as a bedrock to your being. Occasionally withdraw for a period of retreat and recuperation from the world. Solitude brightens our awareness of the ordinary.

The great traditions of fasting and abstinence are powerful tools for creating a freshness to our being. Ramadhan, Lent, Yom Kippur and Native American vision quests are reminders that there is more to life than consumption. In Indonesian culture, if you are discontent with the state of your life you do *prihatin*, the intentional taking on of some small suffering such as fasting or cutting down sleep, to help change your circumstances.

We cannot force ourselves to re-awaken but we can remember to open ourselves to the possibility of each moment. The more we flame the fires of intention, the greater the likelihood that our souls will be filled with unexpected grace. Spirit flows to any place in us that is empty and ready. Then, in the tumult of distracting forces, we hear a still, small voice of inspiration, a guide to the path. This is the sense of 'rightness.' We are attuned to the Greater process.

Finding Our Way

At any moment we are here and nowhere else. Once we realize where 'here' is, we can take the next step. The journey is difficult. It has no end, no fixed goal and each moment is a new, fresh beginning. In order not to wander aimlessly, we need an inner guide, a sense of direction that is not dependent on a fixed objective.

This is *knowing*. Like the beam of a flashlight in the dark of night it illuminates, for a moment, that which it touches and then moves on. The circle of light cannot encompass the whole scene, does not highlight more than a miniscule part, but what it does is bright and clear.

Every aspect of our being, from the tiniest cell to our whole Self, is designed to know.[5] Our bodies know when it is time to eat and sleep, know how to walk, talk and heal. Our hearts know, by feel, the quality of our relationships. Our minds are curious to gain knowledge of everything under the sun. Deeper within we connect to the mythic and symbolic imagination of all humanity, letting us know what it is to be human. Beyond and within all these ways of knowing is a *Greater knowing*, an absolute conviction that comes from connection with the Greater process—the Will of God, Tao, Spirit.

We lose our way not because we do not know, but because we look in too many directions at once. When our being is disorganized, our ability to trust inner knowing is limited. Have you ever been lost in the forest, only minutes away from the path? If you panic, get flustered it only makes matters worse. To find your way back you have to stop, be still, get oriented and decide which is the right direction to take.

Hidden within our being is a *master map*. Sacred teachings, great works of art and psychological writings illuminate this map, activate our inner compass. We know which route to take because we remember the feeling of moving in the right direction. This is inner guidance, knowing when a course of action is **right**.[6]

This is not the 'rightness' that comes from any external source or authority. No book or person commands it. It does not necessarily accord with our hopes or desires. It is the experience of being more fully attuned to the flow of the universe at this particular moment. The knowing that an action or attitude is right comes from the whole of who we are as we feel the flow of how everything is meant to be.

Much of the time this subtle sensibility is obscured by confusion, fear and clinging. To know, we have to set aside what we want, become empty and listen with the whole of our being. Then a certainty arises, a counsel as to how to live our lives, how to be, what to do and when to do it.

I have found two facets of knowing to be of special importance. On our life journey, we look into the future to see where we are going, where the path leads. This is the guiding principle for our life, what I call *vision*. Then, as we tread the path, we decide when to turn, when to speed up or slow down, when to do or refrain from doing. This is how we fit our actions into the flow of time, what I call *timeliness*. Both vision and timeliness are part of knowing how to be in harmony with life.

Vision

Seeing is a natural form of knowing. We look out of our eyes at the universe to behold all that is around us. Our inner vision is similar as we look into the future to envision what it may hold. Vision, both outer and inner, is a creative process. It does not simply record what is there, it enhances, articulates and creates a pathway for action. Inner vision does not constrain the outcome into a preplanned goal. It opens up possibilities along a particular route, a shining light of knowing within the darkness of the unknown.

When our family was living in a little house in an English village, the rain falling while we snuffled through endless colds, we envisioned a more conducive place to live. That vision was detailed, yet fluid enough that it could have been many places in the world. We visited New Zealand, but from the moment of stepping off the plane we knew this was not it. Eventually, after more searching, we arrived by accidental design in Boulder. This was the right place. Now all we had to do was find the right home.

Two years later, on a snowy winter day we traveled miles up a dirt road to check out a small and neat gabled house high on a mountain ridge. As soon as we stepped inside, we knew we had found it. My son, age four, went up to the owner and asked him, "Can we buy this house to live in?" and we did. Now we look out over the plains from two thousand feet above Boulder, surrounded by pine trees and silence. It matches the vision we invoked those many years ago.

Vision is not extraordinary. When I worked as a carpenter, I learned that before you build anything—a house, a table or a simple box—you have to create an image in your mind. You have to see it from every angle, particularly paying attention to the places where parts are to be attached. Then as you measure, cut and join, the nature of the wood or the demands of the project, force you to adapt and change your simpler plans. The outcome is close to the vision but will always be an adaptation of the plan to reality. Vision is a process of dialogue between the different demands of the inner and outer worlds.

I use vision in psychotherapy. When a client comes to a first session, after half an hour or so, I can usually tell whether therapy will be successful. I discern the whole person behind and within the problems and stuckness. It is as if the consummation of our work together is already present at the beginning of therapy. If I cannot experience that vision, I cannot help.

Vision carries conviction. I have struggled through long and dark years of work with clients, supported by a vision of them complete. Then, almost unexpectedly, that wholeness manifests and the person moves from darkness into light as if it were simply waiting there all the time. The fruit is implicit in each seed, the ending in every beginning. We must learn to envision it.

You have lots of opportunity to practice vision. Every time you go to work, start a project, make a phone call or drive some place, you see the process and the outcome in your minds eye as clearly as you can. Do not force too many details but get a sense of the *best way* in which it can happen.

Examine your life and envision how you would like it to be in a year, five years and even ten years from now. Naturally you cannot account for all the twists and turns. But with vision, there is an inner map that tells you when you are headed in the right direction.

There is a power to envisioning, a power to generate perseverance. Vision focuses intention. While vision gives direction, intention is the driving force that keeps us moving forward. Intention is not 'will.' Will attempts to control the outcome, it won't allow vision to shift and transform. Intention is willingness rather than willfulness. We stay receptive and accept the mysterious way in which things happen. Vision directs; intention propels.

As you create your own vision, notice the quality of your motivation. Are you willing to allow your vision to be realized however that happens? Or are you trying to constrain it all, not only the goal but also the route to that goal? Honing your intention means letting go of control and surrendering to the way things are, rather than how you think they should be.

Envisioning is a process. As we hold the vision, we test our intention against a sense of rightness.[7] This rightness is the flow of the Greater process, the Will of God. It is the way things are and should be, the most fluent path for a process to flow toward wholeness. If we do not keep testing our intention, keep checking the direction of our vision, we become lost. Envisioning requires patience and a sense of the necessary unfolding of time.

Timeliness

I still have a difficult time with patience. I constantly have to remind myself to slow down and pay attention to the dance of time. To live properly requires sensitivity to the directives of each moment. 'Patience' for me has gained a profound meaning, a sense of timeliness that is a key to all actions.[8] Timeliness hangs in that infinitely acute balancing point between forcing the issue and procrastinating. My tendency is to push at time, to make things happen too soon. In the past I would put things off and so lose precious opportunities. Timeliness does neither. It knows when an action is in rhythm with how things unfold.

Timely action is both patient and decisive. If we are rushed and impulsive, we may know what needs to be done but intervene too soon. If we are too slow and apathetic, the moment passes us by. When we are timely, our actions respond to the moment and its intrinsic necessities. We act because the time is ripe.

If we look at the universe, everything has its own time, its own place in the scheme of things:

For everything there is a season, and a time for every
matter under heaven:
a time to be born, and a time to die;
a time to plant, and a time to pluck up what is
planted;
a time to kill, and a time to heal;
a time to break down, and a time to build up...[9]

Ecclesiastes, the Preacher, reminds us that every process comes and goes to its own inherent rhythm. A wise part of us knows how to be present with time, to sense the flow of process. The time to act is always in the continuous *now*. Timeliness senses when that now has arrived.

Nature teaches timeliness. Every year I try to judge when it is the right time to plant the various vegetables in my garden. Every spring is different in the mountains of Colorado. Sometimes I can get a few weeks more growth and sometimes every seedling is wiped out by frost or a foot of snow. If I put off the planting until it is too late and the growing season is short, drought and sunburn will take their toll. I try to get the timing right.

Human beings teach timeliness. I have found through hard experience that therapy clients do not change until they are ready. No matter how much I push, no matter how effective my technique, all I create is more resistance. A stuck client cannot give up her stuckness until her whole self permits it. I must stay tuned to her distinctive process with its own pace and quality. It will tell me when she is prepared to take the next step forward.

Sensing how each action fits naturally into its place in time allows even the simplest activity to go more smoothly. Cleaving a log with the grain, the wood splits effortlessly. Timeliness is a sharp blade of awareness. We must hone that blade on the whetstone of our experience.

Do you push when you are not ready? Do you expect to keep up with some idealized image of how fast others do things? Do you procrastinate or put things out of your mind because they make you uneasy? Life will treat you with respect only as much as you treat time respectfully. With vision and timeliness we embark on a voyage of discovery.

Surrendering to the Way

Life is an unfolding journey of countless steps towards a mysterious destination. How are we to tread the path? Little by little, as we shed encumbrances, we travel lighter. Our self becomes both less and more—less separated and disconnected, more whole and connected. We do not simply skate on the surface of life. We listen intently to inner guidance that leads us onward to the unexpected and extraordinary. We surrender to the way.

Let me illustrate with a story. Once I set out on a lone hitchhiking trip around Scotland. With little money and no objective, I wanted to let the moment guide me. I rested for awhile on an old stone footbridge within mossy Birnam Wood, the forest whose magic motion portends the death of Shakespeare's Macbeth.[10] There I mapped the stirrings of my experience, feeling into the quality of the ancient silence.

Days later, far from any tree, on a bleak and empty mountainside, sleety snow chilled me to the bone. Searching for a disappearing footpath, I trudged through the gathering gloom. I was lost. Images of death by exposure and tragic headlines flitted through my mind—yet beneath it all remained the quiet certainty of protection. As night fell, I came upon a tiny empty hostel, miles from human habitation.

The next morning, waking from a weariness-drugged sleep, I stepped into a regal vision. A court of blood-red deer encircled the cabin, haloed in sunlight dazzling off fallen snow. My struggle was rewarded. I was in exactly the right place.

I tramped empty roads, took rides to unknown places, boarded rural trains to villages whose name caught my fancy. By happenstance I arrived at the town of Oban. It dawned on me that, like many before me, I had been journeying in pilgrimage to the holy isle of Iona.

Sheets of rain accompanied me across the barren width of Mull. Yet as I took the ferry to Iona a beam of sunlight burst out of dark clouds, illuminating the tiny island. I visited the lonely pebble beach where Saint Columba beached his frail *curragh* with twelve monks from Ireland, bringing devotion to a savage land. Signs of ancient habitation and piety were everywhere. In the windswept graveyard lay the remains of King Macbeth.

The Iona spiritual community invited me into the ancient monastery founded by the Irish Saint. I joined them in their services, partook of Holy Communion of white Wonder Bread. In that loving atmosphere I felt the true meaning of spiritual connection and communion. It was as though I again snuggled in the lap of Mother Columba, the nun whose love protected me as a child. On that barren piece of land, out in the northern sea, I was wrapped in the same loving presence.

Each of us is on a pilgrimage to our own sacred isle. It quietly draws us toward tranquility and wholeness. If we let go of striving and clinging, surrender in each moment, we will come upon it unexpectedly. Then we experience a sacred treasure, an all-embracing, mysterious transcendence that can never be depleted.

This transcendence is always available, waiting for us to notice, to come home. We know it in times of serenity and joy. We find it even in the depths of suffering. It visits us disguised in many forms, often taking the shape of ordinary experience.

In a favorite dream of mine, this Presence appeared as the bountiful, ever-giving mythical "Tree of Life." *I am in an orchard on the old Welsh family estate, Ffrwdgrech, with my father. He wears the familiar long gray beard of my childhood. I know he is the Gardener, a numinous presence come to teach me the art of pruning. In a shadowy grove, he shows me a glimmering tree that droops its delicate limbs like a weeping willow. Interwoven through the hanging limbs, in a loose tapestry, grow radiant flowing green tendrils. We cut and pull out one of these tendrils. He explains, "No matter how much you take, the tree always remains whole."*

Life keeps recalling us to wholeness. Let us listen with every fiber of our being.

These are only hints and guesses,
Hints followed by guesses; and the rest
Is prayer, observance, discipline, thought and action.
The hint half guessed, the gift half understood, is
Incarnation.
—T. S. Eliot (from *The Dry Salvages*)

Notes

Preface

1. Colin Wilson's fascinating exposition of the role of *"The Outsider"* was written while he was still very young and feeling a similar dilemma. See Wilson, 1956.

2. See Koestler, 1978 and Bateson, 1972. Systems thinking draws from the work of many innovative writers starting with Von Bertalanffy, 1968, who developed general systems theory. For an overview see Capra, 1996.

3. The international spiritual association of Subud is based on surrender to God through a spiritual exercise that is received spontaneously. The name Subud is an abbreviation of three Sanskrit-derived words susila, budhi and dharma. Together these stand for the qualities of a true human being who is able to surrender to and receive guidance from God in order to follow his or her true path in life that is in accordance with the will of God.

4. Transpersonal psychology emerged out of a sense of the limitations of the humanistic approach to human beings. As such it concerns itself with the ultimate possibilities of human development as recognized in the wisdom traditions of the world. Many profound thinkers have made their way to this burgeoning field of psychology. Abraham Maslow, among others, was instrumental in starting the Journal of Transpersonal Psychology which publishes work by such authors as Ken Wilber, Stanislav Grof and Charles Tart.

Introduction

1. Quoted in Easwaran, 1997, p. 1.

2. Easwaran, 1997, p. 11.

3. This is what Gregory Bateson, a brilliant thinker, called "the pattern which connects." See Bateson, 1972 and Capra, 1988.

4. In his essay, *Foundations of a Person-Centered Approach* (Rogers, 1980), Carl Rogers says, "I wish to point to two related tendencies which have acquired more and more importance in my thinking as the years have gone by. One of these is the actualizing tendency, a characteristic of organic life. One is a formative tendency in the universe as a whole." (P.114). The actualizing tendency is a directional process in life, "an underlying flow of movement toward constructive fulfillment of its inherent possibilities." The formative tendency is, "the ever operating trend toward increased order and interrelated complexity evident at both the organic and inorganic level." (p.126).

5. Keen, 1994, p. 291.

Chapter 1: The Gift of Experience

1. These ideas are the foundation of a phenomenological existentialist approach to epistemology. For further background, consult the works of the existentialist philosophers, particularly Gabriel Marcel, Martin Buber and Maurice Merleau-Ponty.

2. For a brilliant essay on the distinction between explicit and tacit knowing, see Polanyi, 1966.

3. I am using process in a philosophically similar way to that of Alfred North Whitehead. In *Process and Reality*, his ninth "category of explanation" determines: "That *how* an actual entity *becomes* constitutes what that actual entity *is*; so that the two descriptions of an actual entity are not independent. Its 'being' is constituted by its 'becoming.' This is the 'principle of process.'"—Whitehead, 1929, P.28.

4. Arnold Mindell, who has developed a comprehensive psychotherapeutic system called "Dreambody Work" or "Process Psychology", uses a similar yet different approach to process. Mindell says, "I use the word process to refer to changes in perception, to the variation of signals experienced by an observer. The observer's personality determines which signals he picks up, which he is aware of and which he identifies himself with and therefore which he reacts to." (Mindell, 1985, p. 11.). Mindell's system is complex and multifaceted and requires study and training to master.

5. See Capra, 1982, for an overview of the new scientific paradigm. He uses a systems model to explore inter-relatedness and interdependence. General systems theory is an overarching conceptual framework first articulated by Ludwig Von Bertalanffy. Von Bertalanffy was closely connected with a new trend in scientific epistemology characterized by information theory, cybernetics and Korzybski's general semantics. Systems theory has given us useful concepts such as emergence, homeostasis, equifinality and system boundaries. Although some of these ideas have been seen to be somewhat mechanical and limited in scope, his influence on scientific explanation has been immense.

6. For an overview of 'new science' ideas see Capra, 1996 and Combs, 1996.

7. Holism, the basic concept of wholes and parts, was developed by Jan Smuts, Prime Minister of South Africa during the early part of the twentieth century. His book *Holism and Evolution* published in 1926 had a profound influence on many systems thinkers and innovative psychologists including Fritz Perls.

Chapter 2: Process: The Flow of Life

1. Jean Piaget, the foremost developmental psychologist, used the term 'object constancy' to describe the progressive development of knowledge in the baby that things and people remain relatively the same over time.

2. The 'stream of consciousness' was so named by the great American psychologist, William James.

3. Alfred North Whitehead, the great philosopher, tells us, "the human intellect 'spatializes the universe'; that is to say that it tends to ignore the fluency, and to analyze the world in terms of static categories." —Whitehead, 1929, p. 242.

4. "Without doubt, if we are to go back to that ultimate, integral experience, unwarped by the sophistication of theory, that experience whose elucidation is the final aim of philosophy, the flux of things is one ultimate generalization around which we must weave our philosophical system."—Whitehead, 1929, p. 240.

5. What Heraclitus said actually translates as, "Upon those who step into the same rivers flow other and yet other waters."—Melchert, 1995 Vol. I, p16. Alfred North Whitehead includes all experience in a similar assertion: "The ancient doctrine that 'no one crosses the same river twice' is extended. No thinker thinks twice; and, to put the matter more generally, no subject experiences twice." —Whitehead, 1929, p. 34.

6. Melchert, 1995, Vol. I, p.16.

7. Clarkson, 1993.

8. Melchert, 1995, Vol. I, p. 17.

9. I will be using the term *Life Force* in a similar manner to Physis. It parallels but is more encompassing than the *élan vital* of Henri Bergson. The "Life Force" may be thought of as the "formative tendency", Aristotelian *entelechy*, the *Holy Spirit* of Christianity, the Kabbalistic *Shekinah*, the *Roh Illofi* of mystical Islam or any other purposive transcendent impetus that breathes life into the lifeless and draws evolution toward more complexity and integration. I prefer the more animistic and teleological "Life Force" to the more scientific term "attractor", which seems to serve a similar function. For an exposition of these concepts, see Allan Combs, 1996.

10. See Lama Anagarika Govinda in the preface to Blofeld, 1965.

11. Quoted in Blofeld, 1965, p. 31.

12. See Waysun Liao, 1977, for a concise explanation of Yin, Yang and their relationship with Ch'i, life energy. He says, "The human being, also a part of the universe, is powered by the same force of energy—ch'i. The process of human life is based on the interaction of Yin and Yang forces. Our life increases and changes, and for reasons that are still mysterious to us, it follows a natural cycle and eventually dies. Ancient Chinese explain this cycle as the growth and fading of ch'i. It is ch'i that determines human mental and physical conditions. The way in which ch'i is expressed is commonly known as the *nature* of things."—Liao, 1977. p. 33.

13. Hua-Ching, 1979, p16.

14. Bohm, 1980, p. 11. Bohm's thinking is complex and somewhat impenetrable for a non-physicist. However, the concepts of the

"implicate and explicate" order of the universe essentially mirrors Tao and Teh (the manifest universe) in the Chinese system.

15. "Not only is everything changing, but all *is* flux. That is to say, *what is* is the process of becoming itself, while all objects, events, entities, conditions, structures, etc., are forms that can be abstracted from this process."—Bohm, 1980, p. 48.

16. Huxley, 1954, p. 23.

17. "There is nothing that stands fast, nothing fixed, nothing free from change, among the things which come into being, neither among those in heaven nor among those on earth. God alone stands unmoved." —Hermes Trismegistus, from Hermetica, quoted in Perry, 1971, p. 773.

18. For an accessible and interesting discussion about the nature of life, see Capra, 1996.

19. See Sheldrake, 1991, p. 99: "life involves both an energy flow, which can be understood as an aspect of the universal flux, and a formative principle, which gives an organism the ends to which its life processes are attracted."

20. Erich Jantsch explains that recent models of life all have similar themes. "(These) may be summarized by notions such as self-determination, self-organization and self-renewal; by a recognition of a systemic interconnectedness over space and time of all natural dynamics; by the logical supremacy of processes over spatial structures; . . .by the openness and creativity of an evolution which is neither in its emerging or decaying structures, nor in the end result, predetermined." —Jantsch, 1980, p. 8.

21. The unpredictable yet directional nature of life can be explained in terms of "strange attractors." This "strange attraction" is not simple, linear or determined; it tends to, "exist *on the edge of chaos*" —Combs, 1996, p. 31.

22. See Jantsch, 1980.

23. Mihaly Csikszentmihalyi has explored the concept of flow, "the total involvement with life" in great depth, (1990 and 1997). He describes flow as an optimal experience that is directed toward some specific goal: "If a person sets out to achieve a difficult enough goal, from

which all other goals logically follow, and if he or she invests all energy in developing skills to reach that goal, then actions and feelings will be in harmony, and the separate parts of life will fit together . . ." (1990, p. 214). While I agree with most of Csikszentmihalyi's rationalist exposition, I experience flow somewhat differently. Flow, in its greater manifestation, is goal-less and does not require willful effort. It manifests through alignment with the way everything, the whole universe flows.

24. Sumohadiwidjojo, 1990, chapter 6.

Chapter 3: The Dimensions of Process

1. This is the title of a series of talks by Bapak Muhammad Subuh Sumohadiwidojo. See *Bapak's Talks*, Subud Publications International Ltd.

2. Of the dimensions of process I capitalize the "Greater" process because it is all encompassing.

3. See Rushforth, 1981.

4. The outer process is similar to an extroverted mode of being in C. G. Jung's terminology. It also has some relationship to what he termed the Persona, that structure of the personality that is used to deal with the world. Outer process has no structure but is a constantly evolving pattern of relationship with the world. See Jung, 1971.

5. The inner process has some similarities to Jung's introverted mode of being (Jung, 1971). It does not correspond to any particular aspect of his structural model of the self. The inner process is a constantly evolving recursive pattern of relationship with itself, out of which emerges the sense of the personal or subjective self.

6. The deeper process is not identical with either a Freudian or Jungian unconscious. I use the term 'unconscious' as a descriptive and not a structural concept, in a similar way to Milton Erickson. All experience that is beyond awareness is unconscious. The deeper process includes: bodily processes; schemas, archetypes, instincts that structure other processes; repressed and forgotten experiences; potentials and unrealized possibilities; over-learned programs of behavior such as walking, talking, etc.; dreams, fantasies and imaginings; and more of

which we are unawares.

7. The Greater process has some similarities with Assagioli's super-conscious or certain aspects of Jung's collective unconscious and even "cosmic consciousness." However, it is not a structure or simply an aspect of our personal experience. It is a different context of experiencing and being. I use the term Greater process for both that aspect of the transpersonal that we can embody (the immanent) and for the totality of all processes (the transcendent). The Greater process is the most subtle and profound manifestation of the Life Force as it moves through our being.

Chapter 4: Exploring the Dimensions of Process

1. This goal-oriented approach to spirituality is what Chogyam Trungpa, the Tibetan founder of Naropa University, calls "spiritual materialism." It captures most of us at some time in our journey. See Trungpa, 1973.

2. See the work of Benjamin Libet et al as described by Wolf, 1994, pp. 88 ff.

3. Our sleep cycles every ninety minutes or so through different brain wave patterns. REM is characterized by alpha waves and is closest to waking. The delta pattern occurs during deepest sleep and is associated with physical recuperation and healing. See Varela, (Ed.) 1997, for a fascinating account of discussions of sleep and dreaming with the Dalai Lama.

4. We move in and out of subtly different states of awareness in a rhythmic 90 minute cycle called "ultradian rhythms." See Rossi, 1986.

5. This transitional area between deeper and inner processes is often termed the "subconscious" in popular terminology.

6. I am using *self* here in its ordinary meaning—the sense of coherent individuality that carries our normal and ongoing identity. When self has a small "s" it corresponds to the ego or "I-ness," sometimes called the small self. When "Self" is capitalized, it refers to the totality of all aspects of that person, both conscious and unconscious. This is similar to Jungian usage, though often he calls the self the *ego*. It is interesting to note that Freud did not use the term ego but used the German for "I." For a comprehensive discussion of the self, see Young-Eisendrath and Hall,

(eds.), 1987 and Glover, 1988.

7. Technically, we speak of some thought or feeling as being ego-syntonic (acceptable to the self) or ego-dystonic (unacceptable to the self).

8. See Jung, 1971.

9. Rushforth, 1985.

10. When I speak of 'human beings' and being 'human', I do so in the sense of a goal toward which we are moving. I do not believe that greed, selfishness, violence and destruction are human. That means that much of our behavior is sub-human.

11. See Rossi and Cheek, 1988, who detail many ideodynamic methods of accessing unconscious information.

Chapter 5: The Thread of Life

1. I am unable to trace down a reference for the concept of the "long body." A friend who had been a follower of Gurdjieff and Ouspensky for many years related it to me. G. I. Gurdjieff was a powerful and charismatic spiritual teacher in the early part of the 20th century. There are many books and study groups based on his ideas. See, for example, Kenneth Walker, 1957, A Study of Gurdjieff's Teaching, London, Jonathan Cape.

2. Anyone concerned with self-knowledge owes a great debt to Socrates. He believed that, "The unexamined life is not worth living."

3. David Cheek has used hypnotic techniques to explore interuterine experience and knowing. See Rossi and Cheek, 1988.

4. "Rebirthing", or re-experiencing of the birth process, can be evoked through breath techniques (such as Holotrophic Breathing developed by Stanislav Grof), hypnosis and various kinds of psychological bodywork.

5. Many traditional cultures—ancient Hebrew, African and Native American for example—venerate and recognize the power of the ancestors. Whether we take the concept of ancestors as a metaphorical description of all those influences that come from ancestry or as spirit entities who are inextricably joined to us, is a matter of belief. For an African viewpoint see, Somé, 1994.

6. Many writers, for example Arthur Koestler, 1978, believe that our

brain and our nature are constructed in layers. Upon the reptilian brainstem sits the mammalian mid brain. The later human cortex covers it all. Our 'higher functions' are often at the mercy of more primitive forces within us.

7. Rudolf Steiner, a practical mystic, started the Waldorf educational movement in Germany at the end of the last century that now has schools in most countries of the world. He believed that a child's education should be in accord with emotional, physical, intellectual and spiritual developmental needs.

8. Lois Cusick, *Waldorf Parenting Handbook*, 1979, p. 37, New York, St. George Publications.

9. Freud called this period of development "latency" with the assumption that sexuality was dormant. His ideas require modification in the light of research and our real experience (I don't remember being dormant!). However, there is some sense that this period is less explicitly complicated than either earlier or later.

10. When I use the term "marriage" in this section it is in its inclusive definition as a 'joining in intimate relationship.' It does not assume the sex or sexuality of the partners.

11. Keen, 1983.

12. Sam Keen, 1983, tells us that to be a 'lover' is the pinnacle of human growth. It connects the human and the transcendent within a *Passionate Life*.

13. See endnote 2.

Chapter 6: Vulnerability and Resilience

1. Temperament has been studied in great depth and over long periods, particularly in studies comparing twins reared together and apart. See, for example, Plomin and Dunn, 1986.

2. Carl Waddington, 1977, tells us that the continuing argument of nature versus nurture is empty—it has little real meaning. There can be no genotype without a phenotype and no phenotype without a genotype; it is a total transactional process. This is the foundation of his "epigenetics", the gene/environment pathway or *chreod* of process.

3. See Flach, 1988. Although he takes a structural approach to resilience in terms of personality traits rather than processes, Flach's definitions are useful (see P. xii).

4. See Winnicot, 1964.

5. See Aron, 1996.

6. See Herman, 1992. This is an excellent overview of the subject of trauma and recovery.

7. I am using "compensation" in an Adlerian and osteopathic sense. Adler, one of the close disciples of Freud, believed that part of our need for power is expressed through compensation and over-compensation for any inferiorities, particularly physical (he was a small man). Osteopaths, working with the structural and spinal system of the body, note that when there is an injury causing structural weakness, the system adapts itself around that vulnerability to minimize its impact.

8. I make a distinction between *turbulence*, which are unpredictable and disturbing life events, and *turmoil*, which is disturbed and disordered experiential process.

9. The new science of *chaos theory* shows us that chaos often exists in the transition between one kind of order or pattern to another.

10. Flach, 1988, p. 14.

11. See Jung, 1971.

12. Her life story is to be published shortly under her real name.

13. As Frederic Flach says, "Resilience is not an exclusively interior quality. Its existence, growth, and survival depend significantly on what and who fills the space around us and the nature of the balance that exists between ourselves and the outer world."—Flach, 1988, p. 209.

14. Flach, 1988, outlines the main personality traits that he believes contribute to resilience: strong self-esteem, independence of thought and action, balanced personal relationships, personal discipline and responsibility, open-mindedness, a willingness to dream, humor, a wide range of interests, self-insight, tolerance of distress, commitment to a meaningful framework of life. See Flach, 1988, p. 113-114.

15. The terminology, *internal and external locus of control* was first

coined by Julian Rotter but has given rise to a large number of psychological studies. "Internals" have been observed to do better in school, to be more independent, to be more able to delay gratification, and to be better at coping with various stresses.

16. A fascinating approach to trauma resolution, developed by Peter Levine, is called *somatic experiencing*. He argues that trauma is locked into the body through the inherent somatic response of freezing when threatened. See Levine, 1997.

17. EMDR, *Eye Movement Desensitization and Reprocessing*, was developed by Francine Shapiro in the 1980's. Since then many thousands of therapists have been trained as it has been found to be extremely effective in resolving trauma and emotionally charged experiences. See Shapiro, 1997. I prefer to use rhythmic alternating sound and sensation rather than eye movements in my practice.

18. See Mindell, 1985.

19. This metaphor is explored with brilliance and profound meaning in Doris Lessing's, *The Marriages between Zones Three, Four, and Five*, (1980, London, Grafton Books) which is part of her *Canopus in Argos: Archives* series.

20. Victor Frankl's work has had a profound influence on existentialist psychotherapy or what he termed "Logotherapy." A good introduction is the classic *The Doctor and the Soul*, Frankl, 1955.

21. Rushforth,1984, p. 171. Winifred completed her autobiography, *Ten Decades of Happenings*, just before she died.

22. Ibid., p. 175.

Chapter 7: Suffering

1. There is much controversy around the validity and reality of recovered memories of sexual abuse. The parents of Jennifer Freyd, a psychologist, set up a lobbying organization called the "False Memory Syndrome Foundation" after she purportedly recovered memories of being sexually abused by her father. See Freyd, 1993. For an overview of the debate see Toon et al, 1996.

2. Isabel Duffy, personal communication.

3. God grant me the serenity to accept the things I cannot change, the courage to change the things I can, and the wisdom to know the difference. See Hemfelt & Fowler, 1990.

4. The diagnosis of *adjustment disorder* is a favorite of psychotherapists using the DSM IV (Diagnostic and Statistical Manual of the American Psychiatric Association). It essentially means that a person is profoundly unhappy because of their circumstances, but carries an assumption that unless we "adjust" to our situation we have a psychiatric disorder.

5. "In the *Inferno* divine retribution assumes the form of the *contrapasso*, i.e., the just punishment of sin, effected by a process either resembling or contrasting to the sin itself."—Mack et al., 1973, p.860.

6. "Logo therapy", developed by Victor Frankl, is based on the search for meaning and purpose within even the most desperate situations. See Frankl, 1955.

7. There are some fascinating video observations by Ray Birdwhistle in the study of "Kinesics" that show cultural and family differences in patterns of movement by age three.

8. For an interesting critique of the influence of Descartes on Western thinking, watch the video *Mindwalk*, written by Fritjof Capra.

9. I am using *It* in the same way as Martin Buber, 1958, and in contrast to *Thou*. The I-It relationship is alienated, instrumental and *thing* oriented; the I-Thou relationship is intimate, connected and process oriented.

10. This is a loose adaptation of some of the ideas in *object relations theory*. Basically, object relations theory suggests that our relationship with the important 'objects' (i.e., people) of our childhood sets the scene for how our self becomes structured, and determines our pattern of relations with the world. I basically agree with this idea but do not like the static terminology—object, structure, etc. There are no 'objects' in the psyche, just processes that are ongoing patterns of relatedness.

11. This incident could be seen as an example of the way in which small initial differences in complex systems can lead to overwhelming

results—the butterfly's flight giving rise to a hurricane.

12. Quoted in Easwaran, 1977, p. 43.

13. This ability of living systems to generate many different processes that lead to the same end is termed *equifinality* in general systems theory. See Von Bertalanffy, 1968.

14. In systems terms, *stuckness* is a failure in the basic processes of self-organization. Living systems exist as enduring patterns of process, far from equilibrium. Stuckness is a looping of negative feedback processes which creates pockets of static 'closedness' in an otherwise open system.

15. I am using the word *reality* to stand in for "the way everything is and will be." In that sense there are multiple realities that are nested within each other, each with their own necessities and "laws." So the outer process reflects the realities of the outer world, which are quite different from the realities of the inner or deeper worlds. Each is a domain that has its own 'language', logic and coherence, each of which must be adhered to and worked with. It is psychotic to bring the rules of the deeper world to that of the outer—we then live a dream and not a life. Similarly the inner world is not 'rational': *the heart has reasons that reason cannot know.*

16. Freud believed that there were two inherent and conflicting forces in the psyche, Eros and Thanatos. Eros is the force of life and connection; Thanatos is the death instinct. If we put this in nonlinear terms we see that there is a constant cyclical relationship between the forces of self-organization/negentrophy and the forces of decomposition/entropy. Life requires death, just as death requires life.

Chapter 8: Connection and Wholeness

1. "If the doors of perception were cleansed every thing would appear to man as it is, infinite." This is a famous quotation from William Blake that was used in the title of the book *Doors of Perception* by Aldous Huxley, 1954.

2. Freud called this process of imbuing things with energy, attractiveness and interest, "cathexis." I think of cathexis as the way in which we create an energetic connection to whatever captures our attention.

3. 'Human beings cannot not communicate', is a central tenet of the work of Ruesch and Bateson, 1951. This is the same as saying that human beings must always be in relationship.

4. In systems theory this is called 'emergence.' Out of the systemic interrelationship of parts, new and unpredictable phenomena arise. See Bateson, 1972 or Von Bertalanffy, 1968,.

5. See Salzberg, 1997.

6. "Whatever a person loves, whether duty, human beings, art, friends, an ideal, or his fellow creatures, he has assuredly opened the door through which he must pass in order to reach that love which is God."—Khan, 1997, p. 87.

7. See Rogers, 1961 and 1980.

8. The terminology "therapeutic container" comes mainly from the work of Jung, particularly his alchemical ideas. It also appears in a slightly different form in the work of early Object Relations theorists such as Bion and Winnicot.

9. I use "chaotic" as it relates to the new science of chaos. It seems that out of chaos arises creative and innovative forms. See Combs, 1996.

10. For a transpersonal approach to relationship, see Welwood, 1996.

11. See Stone and Stone, 1993, for an accessible approach to, *Embracing Your Inner Critic*.

12. The personal *shadow* in Jungian thought is all those aspects of our person that are pushed down into the unconscious. Jung believed that there is not only a personal shadow but also collective shadows belonging to every group of people—to races, societies and to human beings as a whole. As Robert Johnson tells us in his book, *Owning Your Own Shadow*, "To honor and accept one's own shadow is a profound spiritual discipline. It is whole-making and thus holy and the most important experience of a lifetime."—Johnson, 1991, p. x. See also Zeig & Abrams, 1991.

13. For an interesting exploration of "*Symbolic Incest and the Journey Within.*"—Perkins, 1993.

14. This is the inner meaning of the Jewish kosher or Islamic halal

laws for the killing of animals.

15. Carlos Castenada, in his controversial writings about the Yaqui Indian shaman, Don Juan, tells us we should live with the awareness of death always at our left shoulder. See also the section, *The Practice of Dying*, in Singer, 1990, p.157.

16. The term Gaia was coined by James Lovelock to capture the wisdom and connected wholeness of our world ecology.

17. Leonard, 1978, p. xii.

18. McNamara, 1990, p. 108.

19. The anonymous *Way of a Pilgrim*, is a classic description of the benefits of the constant repetition of the "Jesus Prayer": "Lord Jesus Christ, have mercy on me." See Savin, 1991, *The Way of a Pilgrim*. "Centering Prayer", in which the practitioner repeats a spiritually meaningful word or phrase has been popularized by the Cistercian monk, Father Thomas Keating. See Keating, 1986. The Sufi "dhikr" is the constant repetition of "La ilaha illa Allah": "There is no God but God." See Valiuddin, 1980.

20. The form we make of the Greater process is both personal and cultural. For some it can be a personal God, for others it may be Spirit or Emptiness or Nature. Bapak Muhammad Subuh puts it clearly: "So the way such a person thinks about and visualizes heaven and God will not go beyond the images already residing in his or her brain and heart. . . . God preceded the first things and will outlast the last ones. God is within the deepest things and outside the most outward ones. Therefore, God can't be imagined by the human mind, can't be pictured by the human desires, emotions or heart, for God is ahead [of us] and knows more than we know of Him." *Bapak Talks*, New York, 3 May 1959, MSF Series, September 1998.

21. In the *Practice of the Presence of God*, Brother Lawrence, a seventeenth century Carmelite monk, tells us: "I have given up all my non-obligatory devotions and prayers and concentrate on being always in His holy presence; I keep myself in His presence by simple attentiveness and a loving gaze upon God which I can call the actual presence of God or to put it more clearly, an habitual, silent and secret conversation of the

soul with God."—Delaney, 1977, p68.

Chapter 9: Finding Our Way

1. This is what Edward Edinger calls "inflation" - the ego tries to imperialistically take over the domain of the whole Self. See Edinger, 1992.

2. Feng & English, 1974, p. 48.

3. Joseph Campbell, the greatest 'mythologist' of our time, has written extensively about the symbology of the "Hero's Journey." See Campbell, 1988.

4. Thich Nhat Hanh, the Vietnamese spiritual teacher, tells us, "The root word *buddh* means to wake up, to know, to understand; and he or she who wakes up and understands is called a Buddha. It is as simple as that. The capacity to wake up, to understand, and to love is called Buddha nature." - Tich Nhat Hanh, 1987, p. 13.

5. Gregory Bateson as well as Humberto Maturana and Francisco Varela independently came to a similar conclusion: 'mind' or cognition is inherent in any living system by the nature of its processes of self organization and relationship with its environment. See Capra, 1996, for an overview or Maturana and Varela, 1987, for a more complex exposition of these ideas.

6. For readings on *Inner Knowing*, see Palmer, ed., 1998.

7. In Subud there is a process called "testing" in which a question is posed and a response received through the practice of surrender to the Will of God as experienced in the spiritual exercise or latihan.

8. Bapak, the spiritual guide of Subud, kept reminding us of the three essentials of the spiritual life: patience, trust and submission to the Will of God.

9. Ecclesiastes, 3, from *The Holy Bible*, Revised Standard Version Catholic Edition, London, Catholic Truth Society.

10. Macbeth, Act 4, Scene 1:
Macbeth shall never vanquish'd be until
Great Birnam wood to high Dunsinane hill
Shall come against him.

Bibliography

Almaas, A. H. (1986). *Essence—The Diamond Approach to Inner Realization*. York Beach, ME: Samuel Weiser.

—, (1988). *The Pearl Beyond Price*. Berkley, CA: Diamond Books.

Aron, E. N. (1996). *The Highly Sensitive Person*. A Birch Lane Press Book: Published by Carol Publishing Group.

Bakken, K. L. (1985). *The Call to Wholeness*. New York: The Crossroads Publishing Co.

Bapak's Talks. Volume I. (1993). Rickmansworth, England: Subud Publications International Ltd.

Bateson, G. (1972). *Steps to an Ecology of Mind*. New York: Ballantine Books.

—, (1979). *Mind and Nature*. New York: Bantam.

—, & Bateson, M. C. (1987). *Angels Fear*. London: Rider.

—, (1991). *A Sacred Unity*. "A Cornelia and Michael Bessie Book." An Imprint of HarperCollins Publishers.

Bertalanffy, L. von. (1968). *General System Theory*. New York: George Braziller.

Blofeld, J. (1965). *The Book of Change*. London: George Allen & Unwin Ltd.

Bohm, D. (1980). *Wholeness and the Implicate Order*. London & New York: Ark Paperbacks.

Bois, S. J. (1966). *The Art of Awareness*. Dubuque, Iowa: Wm. C. Brown Company Pubs.

Buber, M. (1958). *I and Thou*. New York: Charles Scribner's Sons.

Campbell, J. (1988). *The Power of Myth*. New York: Doubleday.

Capra, F. (1982). *The Turning Point*. Bantam Books.

—, (1988). *Uncommon Wisdom*. Bantam Books.

—, (1996). *The Web of Life*. Anchor Books: Doubleday.

Carlson, R. & Shield, B., eds. (1989). *Healers on Healing*. Los Angeles: Jeremy P. Tarcher, Inc.

Casement, P. J. (1985). *Learning from the Patient*. New York & London: The Guilford Press.

Clarkson, P. (1993). 2,500 Years of Gestalt: from Heraclitus to the Big Bang. *The British Gestalt Journal*, 2, pp. 4-9.

Clover, J. (1988). *I: The Philosophy and Psychology of Personal Identity*. London: Penguin Books.

Combs, A. (1996). *The Radiance of Being*. St. Paul, MN. Paragon Books.

Csikszentmihalyi, M. (1990). *Flow: The Psychology of Optimal Experience*. New York: Harper & Row.

—, (1997). *Finding Flow*. Basic Books.

Deikman, A. (1982). *The Observing Self*. Boston: Beacon Press.

Delaney, J. J. (1977). *The Practice of the Presence of God by Brother Lawrence of the Resurrection*. New York: Doubleday.

Dennett, D. C. (1991). *Consciousness Explained*. Boston: Little, Brown & Company.

Edinger, F. E. (1992). *Ego and Archetype*. Boston & London: Shambhala.

Eliot, T. S. (1943). *Four Quartets*. New York: A Harvest Book: Harcourt, Brace & World, Inc.

Easwaran, E. (1977). *Gandhi The Man*. Nilgiri Press.

Feng, G & English, J. (trans.). (1974). *Chuang Tsu: Inner Chapters*. London: Wildwood House.

Flach, F. (1988). *Resilience*. New York: Fawcett Columbine.

Frankl, V. E. (1955). *The Doctor and the Soul*. New York: Vintage Books.

Freyd, J. J. (1993). *Theoretical and Personal Perspectives on the Delayed Memory Debate*. A presentation for The Center for Mental Health at Foote Hospital's Continuing Education Conference, Ann Arbor Michigan.

Grof, S. & Bennett, Z. (1992). *The Holotrophic Mind*. San Francisdo. Harper Publications.

Grof, S. (1998). *The Cosmic Game*. Albany, NY. State University of New

York.

Gelberman, Rabbi J. (1978). *Jewish Mysticism.* In Agnihotri, S. N. & O'Brien, J., eds. *Faces of Meditation.* Pennsylvania: Himalayan International Institute.

Glover, J. (1988). *I: The Philosophy and Psychology of Personal Identity.* Penguin Books.

Goldstein, J. & Kornfield, J. (1987). *Seeking the Heart of Wisdom.* Boston & London: Shambhala.

Harper, R. (1991). *On Presence.* Philadelphia: Trinity Press International.

Hayward, J. W. (1984). *Perceiving Ordinary Magic.* Boulder & London: New Science Library, Shambhala.

Heider, J. (1985). *The Tao of Leadership.* New York: Bantam Books.

Hemfelt, R. & Fowler, R. (1990). *Serenity: A Companion for Twelve Step Recovery.* Nashville: Thomas Nelson Publishers.

Herman, J. L. (1992). *Trauma and Recovery.* New York: Basic Books.

Hua-Ching, N. (1979). *Complete Works of Lao Tzu.* Malibu, CA: The Shrine of the Eternal Breath of Tao.

Huxley, A. (1954). *The Doors of Perception. Heaven and Hell.* New York: Harper & Row, Publishers.

Inayat Khan, H. (1882). *The Art of Being and Becoming.* New Lebanon: Omega.

Jantsch, E. (1980). *The Self-Organizing Universe.* Oxford: Pergamon Press.

Johnson, D. H. (1989). *Presence.* In Carlson, R. and Shield, B., eds. Healers on Healing. Los Angeles: Jeremy P. Tarcher.

Johnson, R. A. (1991). *Owning Your Own Shadow.* HarperSanFrancisco.

Jung, C. G. (1953-1990). *Collected Works, vols. 1-20.* Princeton, N.J.: Princeton University Press, Bollingen Series XX.

—, (1957). *The Undiscovered Self.* Boston: Little Brown & Company.

—, (1973). *Memories, Dreams and Reflections.* New York: Pantheon Books.

Keating, T. (1986). *Open Mind, Open Heart.* Rockport MA: Element.

Keen, S. (1983). *The Passionate Life.* New York: HarperSanFrancisco.

—, (1994). *Hymns to an Unknown God.* New York: Bantam Books.

Koestler, A. (1978). *Janus: A Summing Up*. Picador.

Leonard, G. (1978). *The Silent Pulse*. Arkana.

Levine, P. A. (1997). *Waking the Tiger*. Berkley California: North Atlantic Books.

Liao, W. (1977). *The Essence of T'ai Chi*. Boston & London: Shambhala.

Mack, M. et al, eds. (1973). *World Masterpieces*. New York: W. W. Norton & Co.

May, R. (1983). *The Discovery of Being*. New York: W. W. Norton & Co.

Maturana, H. R. & Varela, F. J. (1987). *The Tree of Knowledge*. Boston & London: Shambhala.

Melchert, N. (1995). *The Great Conversation: Volumes I & II*. Mountain View, Ca.: Mayfield Publishing Co.

McNamara, W. (1990). *Alive with God*. in Shield, B. & Carlson, R., eds., *For the Love of God*. San Rafael, CA: New World Library.

Mindell, A. (1985). *River's Way*. London and New York: Routledge & Kegan Paul.

Moore, T. (1992). *Care of the Soul*. New York: Harper Collins.

Nhat Hanh, T. (1975). *The Miracle of Mindfulness*. Boston: Beacon Press.

—, (1987). *Being Peace*. Berkeley, California: Parallax Press.

Palmer, H., ed. (1998). *Inner Knowing*. New York: Jeremy P. Tarcher/Putnam.

Perkins, J. (1993). *The Forbidden Self*. Boston & London: Shambhala.

Perry, W. N. (1971). *A Treasury of Traditional Wisdom*. London: George Allen & Unwin Ltd.

Plomin, R. & Dunn, J., eds. (1986). *The study of temperament: Changes, Continuities, and Challenges*. Hillsdale, NJ: Erlbaum.

Polanyi, M. (1966). *The Tacit Dimension*. New York: Anchor Books, Doubleday & Co. Inc.

Poppel, E. (1985). *Mindworks*. Boston: Harcourt Brace Jovanovich, Publishers.

Rogers, C. R. (1961). *On Becoming a Person*. Boston: Houghton Mifflin.

—, (1980). *A Way of Being*. Boston: Houghton Mifflin.

Rossi, E. L. (1986). *The Psychobiology of Mind-Body Healing*. New York: W.

W. Norton & Co.

—, & Cheek, D. B. (1988). *Mind Body Therapy*. New York: W. W Norton & Co.

Ruesch, J. & Bateson, G. (1951). *Communication: The Social Matrix of Psychiatry*. New York: Norton.

Ruhl, J. M. (1996). *Worlds of Illness*. Dissertation submitted to Pacifica Graduate Institute.

Rushforth, W. (1981). *Something is Happening*. London: Gateway Books.

—, (1984). *Ten Decades of Happenings*. London: Gateway Books.

—, (1985). *Life's Currency*. Bath, Great Britain: Gateway Books.

Salzberg, S. (1997). *Loving Kindness*. Boston & London: Shambhala.

Savin, O. (trans). (1991). *The Way of a Pilgrim*. Boston: Shambhala Publications.

Schumacher, E. F. (1978). *A Guide for the Perplexed*. London: Abacus.

Shah, I. (1964). *The Sufis*. London: Jonathan Cape.

Shapiro, F. (1995). *Eye Movement Desensitization and Reprocessing*. New York & London: The Guilford Press.

Sheldrake, R. (1988). *The Presence of the Past*. Times Books.

—, (1991). *The Rebirth of Nature*. New York: Bantam Books.

Singer, J. (1990). *Seeing Through the Visible World*. HarperSanFrancisco.

Smart, N. (1969). *The Religious Experience of Mankind*. Glasgow: Collins Fount Paperbacks.

Somé, M. (1994). *Of Water and the Spirit*. Penguin/Arkana.

Sumohadiwidjojo, Bapak M. S. (1990). *Autobiography*. Subud Publications International.

Thompson, L. (1984). *Mirror to the Light*. London: Coventure.

Toon, K. et al. (1996). Memory or mirage? The FMS debate. *The Psychologist*, February 1996.

Trungpa, C. (1973). *Cutting Through Spiritual Materialism*. Boston: Shambhala

Varela, F. J. (Ed.). (1997). *Sleeping, Dreaming, and Dying*. Boston: Wisdom Publications.

Valiuddin, M. (1980). *Contemplative Disciplines in Sufism*. East-West

233

Publications.

Van Dusen, W. (1972). *The Natural Depth in Man*. New York: Harper & Row.

Waddington, C. H. (1977). *Tools for Thought*. New York: Basic Books.

Welwood, J. (1996). *Love and Awakening*. New York: HarperCollins.

Whitehead, A. N. (1929). *Process and Reality*. New York: The Free Press.

Wilber, K. (1979). *No Boundary*. Boston: New Science Library.

—, (1997). *The Eye of Spirit*. Boston & London: Shambhala.

Wilson, C. (1956). *The Outsider*. London: Picador.

Winnicot, D. W. (1964). *The Child, the Family, and the Outside World*. Merloyd Addison-Wesley Publishing Co. Inc.

Wolf, F. A. (1994). *The Dreaming Universe*. New York. Simon & Schuster.

Wu, J. C. H., trans. (1961). *Tao Teh Ching*. Boston & Shaftesbury: Shambhala.

Young-Eisendrath, P. & Hall, J. A., eds. (1987). *The Book of the Self*. New York and London: New York University Press.

Zweig, C. & Abrams, J., eds. (1991). *Meeting the Shadow*. Los Angeles: Jeremy P. Tarcher, Inc.

Index

Index